LESSONS OF THE WAR WITH SPAIN AND OTHER ARTICLES • MAHAN, A. T. (ALFRED THAYER)

Publisher's Note

Purchase of this book entitles you to a free trial membership in the publisher's book club at www.rarebooksclub.com. (Time limited offer.) Simply enter the barcode number from the back cover onto the membership form on our home page. The book club entitles you to select from millions of books at no additional charge. You can also download a digital copy of this and related books to read on the go. Simply enter the title or subject onto the search form to find them.

Note: This is an historic book. Pages numbers, where present in the text, refer to the first edition of the book and may also be in indexes.

If you have any questions, could you please be so kind as to consult our Frequently Asked Questions page at www.rarebooksclub.com/faqs.cfm? You are also welcome to contact us there.

Publisher: General Books LLC™, Memphis, TN, USA, 2012. ISBN: 9781153811996.

Proofreading: pgdp.net

❧ ❧ ❧ ❧ ❧ ❧ ❧ ❧

Transcriber's Note:

Inconsistent hyphenation in the original document has been preserved.

Obvious typographical errors have been corrected. For a complete list, please see the end of this document 62

Click on the maps to see a larger version.

Lessons of the War with Spain
And Other Articles

Lessons of the War with Spain

And Other Articles

BY

ALFRED T. MAHAN, D.C.L., LL.D.

Captain United States Navy

AUTHOR OF "THE INTEREST OF AMERICA IN SEA POWER," "THE INFLUENCE OF SEA POWER UPON HISTORY, 1660-1783," "THE INFLUENCE OF SEA POWER UPON THE FRENCH REVOLUTION AND EMPIRE," "THE LIFE OF NELSON, THE EMBODIMENT OF THE SEA POWER OF GREAT BRITAIN," AND OF A "LIFE OF FARRAGUT"

BOSTON
LITTLE, BROWN, AND COMPANY
1899

Copyright, 1898, 1899,
By The S.S. McClure Co.
Copyright, 1898,
By Harper and Brothers
Copyright, 1899,
By The North American Review Publishing Co.
Copyright, 1899,
By John R. Dunlap
Copyright, 1899,
By Alfred T. Mahan

All rights reserved
University Press
John Wilson and Son, Cambridge, U.S.A.

[v]

PREFACE

The original intention, with which the leading articles of the present collection were undertaken, was to elicit some of the lessons derivable from the war between the United States and Spain; but in the process of conception and of treatment there was imparted to them the further purpose of presenting, in a form as little technical and as much popular as is consistent with seriousness of treatment, some of the elementary conceptions of warfare in general and of naval warfare in particular. The importance of popular understanding in such matters is twofold. It promotes interest and induces intelligent pressure upon the representatives of the people, to provide during peace the organization of force demanded by the conditions of the nation; and it also tends to avert the unintelligent pressure which, when war exists, is apt to assume [vi] the form of unreasoning and unreasonable panic. As a British admiral said two hundred years ago, "It is better to be alarmed now, as I am, than next summer when the French fleet may be in the Channel." Indifference in times of quiet leads directly to perturbation in emergency; for when emergency comes, indifference is found to have resulted in ignorance, and fear is never so overpowering as when, through want of comprehension, there is no check upon the luxuriance of the imagination.

It is, of course, vain to expect that the great majority of men should attain even an elementary knowledge of what constitutes the strength or weakness of a military situation; but it does not seem extravagant to hope that the individuals, who will interest themselves thus far, may be numerous enough, and so distributed throughout a country, as to constitute rallying points for the establishment of a sound public opinion, and thus, in critical moments, to liberate the responsible authorities from demands which, however unreasonable, no representative government can wholly withstand.

[vii] The articles do not in any sense constitute a series. Written for various occasions, at various times, there is in them no sequence of treatment, or even of conception. Except the last, however, they all have had a common origin in the war with Spain. This may seem somewhat questionable as regards the one on the Peace Conference; but, without assuming to divine all the motives which led to the call for that assembly, the writer is persuaded that between it and the war there was the direct sequence of a corollary to its proposition. The hostilities with Spain brought doubtless the usual train of sufferings, but these were not on such a scale as in themselves to provoke an outcry for universal peace. The political consequences, on the other hand, were much in excess of those commonly resultant from war,—even from maritime war. The quiet, superficially peaceful progress with which Russia was successfully advancing her boundaries in Asia, adding gain to gain, unrestrained and apparently irrestrainable, was suddenly confronted with the appearance of the United [viii] States in the Philippines, under conditions which made inevitable both a continuance of occupancy and a great increase of military and naval strength. This intrusion, into a sphere hitherto alien to it, of a new military power, capable of becoming one of the first force, if it so willed, was momentous in itself; but it was attended further with circumstances which caused Great Britain, and Great Britain alone among the nations of the earth, to appear the friend of the United States in the latter's conflict. How this friendliness was emphasized in the Philippines is a matter of common report.

Coincident with all this, though also partly preceding it, has been the growing recognition by the western nations, and by Japan, of the imminence of great political issues at stake in the near future of China. Whether regarded as a field for commerce, or for the exercise of the varied activities by which the waste places of the earth are redeemed and developed, it is evidently a matter of economical—and therefore of political—importance to civilized nations to prevent the too preponderant control [ix] there of any one of their number, lest the energies of their own citizens be debarred from a fair opportunity to share in these advantages. The present conditions, and the recent manifestations of antagonism and rivalry, are too well known for repetition. The general situation is sufficiently understood, yet it is doubtful whether the completeness and rapidity of the revolution which has taken place in men's thoughts about the Pacific are duly appreciated. They are shown not only by overt aggressive demands of various European states, or by the extraordinary change of sentiment on the subject of expansion that has swept over America, but very emphatically by the fact, little noted yet well assured, that leading statesmen of Japan—which only three years ago warned the United States Government that even the annexation of Hawaii could not by her be seen with indifference—now welcome our presence in the Philippines.

This altered attitude, on the part of a people of such keen intelligence, has a justification which should not be ignored, and a significance [x] which should not be overlooked. It bears vivid testimony to the rate at which events, as well as their appreciation of events and of conditions, have been advancing. It is one of the symptoms of a gathering accord of conviction upon a momentous subject. At such a time, and on such a scene, the sympathetic drawing together of the two great English-speaking nations, intensely commercial and enterprising, yet also intensely warlike when aroused, and which exceed all others in their possibilities of maritime greatness, gave reason for reflection far exceeding that which springs from imaginative calculations of the future devastations of war. It was a direct result of the war with Spain, inevitably suggesting a probable drift towards concurrent action upon the greatest question of the immediate future, in which the influence of force will be none the less real because sedulously kept in the background of controversies. If, however, the organic development of military strength could be temporarily arrested by general agreement, or by the prevalence of an opinion that war is practically a [xi] thing of the past, the odds would be in favor of the state which at the moment of such arrest enjoys the most advantageous conditions of position, and of power already created.

In reproducing these articles, the writer has done a little editing, of which it is needless to speak except in one respect. His views on the utility of coast fortification have met with pronounced adverse criticism in some quarters in England. Of this he has neither cause nor wish to complain; but he is somewhat surprised that his opinions on the subject here expressed are thought to be essentially opposed to those he has previously avowed in his books,—the Influence of Sea-Power upon History, and upon the French Revolution. While wholly convinced of the primacy of the navy in maritime warfare, and maintaining the subordination to it of the elements of power which rest mainly upon land positions, he has always clearly recognized, and incidentally stated, not only the importance of the latter, but the general necessity of affording them the security of fortification, which enables a weaker force to [xii] hold its own against sudden attack, and until relief can be given. Fortifications, like natural accidents of ground, serve to counterbalance superiority of numbers, or other disparity of means; both in land and sea warfare, therefore, and in both strategy and tactics, they are valuable adjuncts to a defence, for they constitute a passive reinforcement of strength, which liberates an active equivalent, in troops or in ships, for offensive operations. Nor was it anticipated that when coast defence by fortification was affirmed to be a nearly constant element, the word "constant" would be understood to mean the same for all countries, or under varying conditions of popular panic, instead of applying to the deliberate conclusions of competent experts dealing with a particular military problem.

Of the needs of Great Britain, British officers should be the best judge, although even there there is divergence of opinion; but to his own countrymen the author would say that our experience has shown that adequate protection of a frontier, by permanent works judiciously planned, conduces to the energetic prosecution of offensive [xiii] war. The fears for Washington in the Civil War, and for our chief seaports in the war with Spain, alike illustrate the injurious effects of insufficient home defence upon movements of the armies in the field, or of the navies in campaign. In both instances dispositions of the mobile forces, vicious from a purely military standpoint, were imposed by fears for stationary positions believed, whether rightly or wrongly, to be in peril.

For the permission to republish these articles the author begs to thank the proprietors of the several periodicals in which they first appeared. The names of these, and the dates, are given, together with the title of each article, in the Table of Contents.

[xiv]
[xv]

Lessons of the War with Spain, 1898.
McClure's Magazine, December, 1898-April, 1899.

		Page
Introductory: Comprehension of Military and Naval Matters possible to the People, and important to the Nation		3 ... 4
I. ... 7	How the Motive of the War gave Direction to its Earlier Movements.—Strategic Value of Puerto Rico.—Considerations on the Size and Qualities of Battleships.—Mutual Relations of Coast Defence and Navy	21 ...7
II. 13	The Effect of Deficient Coast-Defence upon the Movements of the Navy.—The Military and Naval Conditions of Spain at the Outbreak of the War	53 . 13
III. .. 20	Possibilities open to the Spanish Navy at the Beginning of the War.—The Reasons for Blockading Cuba.—First Movements of the Squadrons under Admirals Sampson and Cervera	90 . 20
IV. .. 26	Problems presented by Cervera's Appearance in West Indian Waters.—Movements of the United States Divisions and of the *Oregon*.—Functions of Cruisers in a Naval Campaign	126 26
V. ... 35 [xvi]	The Guard set over Cervera.—Influence of Inadequate Numbers upon the Conduct of Naval and Military Operations.—Cámara's Rush through the Mediterranean, and Consequent Measures taken by the United States	170 35

The Peace Conference and the Moral Aspect of War 41	207

North American Review, October, 1899.

The Relations of the United States to their New Dependencies 47	241

Engineering Magazine, January, 1899.

Distinguishing Qualities of Ships of War 50	257

Scripps-McRae Newspaper League, November, 1898.

Current Fallacies upon Naval Subjects 53	277

Harpers' Monthly Magazine, June, 1898.

[xvii]
MAPS

Island of Cuba	To face page 59 .14
The Caribbean	To

	face page
Sea	113 24

LESSONS OF THE WAR WITH SPAIN

AND OTHER ARTICLES

[3]

LESSONS OF THE WAR WITH SPAIN

INTRODUCTORY

ToC 3

Comprehension of Military and Naval Matters possible to the People, and important to the Nation.

It is somewhat of a commonplace among writers upon the Art of War, that with it, as with Art in general, the leading principles remain unimpaired from age to age. When recognized and truly mastered, not held by a passive acquiescence in the statements of another, but really appropriated, so as to enter decisively into a man's habit of thought, forming in that direction the fibre of his mind, they not only illuminate conditions apparently novel, by revealing the essential analogies between them and the past, but they supply the clue by which the intricacies of the present can best be threaded. Nothing could be more utterly superficial, for instance, than the remark [4] of a popular writer that "the days of tacks and sheets"—of sailing ships, that is—"have no value as lessons for the days of steam and armor." Contrast with such an utterance the saying of the great master of the art,—Napoleon: "If a man will surprise the secrets of warfare, let him study the campaigns of Hannibal and of Cæsar, as well as those of Frederick the Great and my own."

Comprehension of warfare, therefore, consists, first, in the apprehension and acceptance—the mental grasp—of a few simple general principles, elucidated and formulated by admitted authorities upon the subject, and, second, in copious illustration of these principles by the application of them to numerous specific instances, drawn from actual experiences of war—from history. Such illustration, adequately developed by exposition of facts and of principles in the several cases, pointing out, where necessary, substantial identity underlying superficial diversity, establishes gradually a body of precedents, which reinforce, by all the weight of cumulative authority, the principle that they illuminate. Thus is laid the substantial foundation upon which the Art of War securely [5] rests. It is perhaps advisable—though it should be needless—to say that, when a student has achieved such comprehension, when his mind has mastered the principles, and his memory is richly stored with well-ordered precedents, he is, in war, as in all other active pursuits of life, but at the beginning of his labors. He has girded on his armor, but he has not yet proved it,— far less is qualified to boast as one about to put it off after a good life's fight. It remains yet to be seen whether he has the gifts and the manhood to use that which he has laboriously acquired, or whether, as happens with many other men apparently well qualified, and actually well furnished with the raw material of knowledge in various professions, he will be unable to turn power into success. This question trial alone can decide in each individual case; but while experience thus forces all to realize that knowledge does not necessarily imply capacity to use it, that there may be foundation upon which no superstructure will be raised, few—and those not the wisest—are inclined to dispute that antecedent training, well-ordered equipment, where other things are equal, does give a distinct [6] advantage to the man who has received it. The blaze of glory and of success which, after forty years of patient waiting, crowned the last six months of Havelock's life, raising him from obscurity to a place among the immortals, attests the rapidity with which the perfect flower of achievement can bud and fully bloom, when, and only when, good seed has been sown in ground fitly prepared.

There are two principal methods of imparting the illustrations that, in their entirety, compose the body of precedents, by which the primary teachings of the Art of War are at once elucidated and established. By the first, the several principles may be separately stated, more or less at large, each being followed closely by the appropriate illustrations, drawn, as these in such a treatment most suitably may, from different periods and from conditions which on the surface appear most divergent. Or, on the other hand, the consecutive narrative of a particular series of operations may be given, in such detail as is necessary, accompanied by a running commentary or criticism, in which the successive occurrences are brought to the test of recognized standards; inference being [7] drawn, or judgment passed, accordingly. The former is the more formal and methodical; it serves better, perhaps, for starting upon his career the beginner who proposes to make war the profession of his life; for it provides him, in a compact and systematic manner, with certain brief rules, by the use of which he can most readily apply, to his subsequent reading of military history, criteria drawn from the experience of centuries. He is thus supplied, in short, with digested knowledge. But digestion by other minds can in no wise take the place of assimilation performed by one's own mental processes. The cut and dried information of the lecture room, and of the treatise, must in every profession be supplemented by the hard work of personal practice; and failing the experience of the campaign,—of actual warfare,—the one school of progress for the soldier or seaman is to be found in the study of military and naval history, which embodies the experience of others. To such study the second method contributes; it bears to the first the relation of an advanced course.

Nor let it be supposed that the experience of others, thus imparted, is a poor substitute [8] for that acquired by the actual hard work of the field, or of the ocean. By the process, the fruit possibly may not be fully matured; but it arrives at that perfection of form which requires but a few suns to ripen. This, moreover, if not the only way by which experience in the art of directing operations of war—of command-in-chief—can be stored, is by far the most comprehensive and thorough; for while utility cannot be denied to annual manœuvres, and to the practice of the sham battle, it must be remembered that these, dealing with circumstances limited both in time and place, give a very narrow range of observation; and, still more important, as was remarked by the late General Sherman, the moral elements of danger and uncertainty, which count for so much in real warfare, cannot be adequately reproduced in mimic. The field of military history, on the other hand, has no limit short of the military experience of the race; it records the effect of moral influences of every kind, as well as of the most diverse material conditions; the personal observation of even the greatest of captains is in comparison but narrow. "What experience [9] of command," says one of the most eminent, "can a general have, before he is called to command? and the experience of what one commander, even after years of warfare, can cover all cases?" Therefore he prescribes study; and as a help thereto tells the story of one of his most successful campaigns, accompanying it with a commentary in which he by no means spares himself. Napoleon abounds in the same sense. "On the field of battle the happiest inspiration is often but a recollection,"—not necessarily of one's own past; and he admitted in after years that no finer work had been done by him than in his first campaign, to which he came—a genius indeed, but— with the acquisitions chiefly of a student, deep-steeped in reading and reflection upon the history of warfare.

The utility of such study of military history to the intending warrior is established, not only by a few such eminent authorities, but by a consensus among the leading soldiers and seamen of our own day, whether they personally have, or have not, had the opportunity of command in war. It may be asserted to be a matter of contemporary professional [10] agreement, as much as any other current opinion that now obtains. In such study, native individual capacity and individual temperament will largely affect inference and opinion; not only causing them to differ more or less, but resulting frequently in direct opposition of conclusion. It cannot be otherwise; for, like all other callings of active life, war is a matter, not merely of knowledge and of general principles, but of sound judgment, without which both information and rules, being wrongly applied, become useless. Opinions, even of the most eminent, while accorded the respect due to their reputation, should therefore be brought to the test of personal reflection.

The study of the Art and History of War is pre-eminently necessary to men of the profession, but there are reasons which commend it also, suitably presented, to all citizens of our country. Questions connected with war—when resort to war is justifiable, preparation for war, the conduct of war—are questions of national moment, in which each voter—nay, each talker—has an influence for intelligent and adequate action, by the formation of sound public opinion; and public opinion, in [11] operation, constitutes national policy. Hence it is greatly to be desired that there should be more diffused interest in the critical study of warfare in its broader lines. Knowledge of technical details is not necessary to the apprehension of the greater general principles, nor to an understanding of the application of those principles to particular cases, when made by individual students,—officers or others. The remark is sometimes heard, "When military or naval officers agree, Congress—or the people—may be expected to act." The same idea applied to other professions—waiting for universal agreement—would bring the world to a standstill. Better must be accepted without waiting for best. Better is more worth having to-day than best is the day after the need has come and gone. Hesitation and inaction, continued till the doctors agree, may result in the death of the patient; yet such hesitation is almost inevitable where there is no formed public opinion, and quite inevitable where there is no public interest antecedent to the emergency arising.

It may be due to the bias of personal or professional inclination that the present [12] writer believes that military history,—including therein naval,— simply and clearly presented in its leading outlines, divested of superfluous and merely technical details, would be found to possess an interest far exceeding that which is commonly imagined. The logical coherence of any series of events, as of any process of Nature, possesses an innate attraction for the inquisitive element of which few intelligent minds are devoid. Unfortunately, technical men are prone to delight in their technicalities, and to depreciate, with the adjective "popular," attempts to bring their specialties within the comprehension of the general public, or to make them pleasing and attractive to it. However it may be with other specialties, the utility of which is more willingly admitted, the navy and army in our country cannot afford to take such an attitude. The brilliant, but vague, excitement and glory of war, in its more stirring phases, touches readily the popular imagination, as does intense action of every description. It has all the charm of the dramatic, heightened by the splendor of the heroic. But where there is no appeal beyond the imagination to the intellect, such [13] impressions lack distinctness, and leave no really useful results. While there is a certain exaltation in sharing, through vivid narrative, the emotions of those who have borne a part in some deed of conspicuous daring, the fascination does not equal that wrought upon the intellect, as it traces for the first time the long-drawn sequence by which successive occurrences are seen to issue in their necessary results, or causes apparently remote to converge upon a common end, and understanding succeeds to the previous sense of bewilderment, which is produced by military events as too commonly treated.

There is, moreover, no science—or

art—which lends itself to such exposition more readily than does the Art of War. Its principles are clear, and not numerous. Outlines of operations, presented in skeleton, as they usually may be, are in most instances surprisingly clear; and, these once grasped, the details fall into place with a readiness and a precision that convey an ever increasing intellectual enjoyment. The writer has more than once been witness of the pleasure thus occasioned to men wholly strangers to military matters; a pleasure [14] partly of novelty, but which possesses the elements of endurance because the stimulus is one that renews itself continually, opening field after field for the exercise of the mind.

If such pleasure were the sole result, however, there might be well-founded diffidence in recommending the study. The advantage conferred upon the nation by a more wide-spread and intelligent understanding of military matters, as a factor in national life that must exist for some ages to come, and one which recent events, so far from lessening, have rendered more conspicuous and more necessary, affords a sounder ground for insisting that it is an obligation of each citizen to understand something of the principles of warfare, and of the national needs in respect of preparation, as well as thrill with patriotic emotion over an heroic episode or a brilliant victory.

It is with the object of contributing to such intelligent comprehension that the following critical narrative, which first appeared in one of our popular monthlies, is again submitted to the public in its present form. It professes no more than to be an attempt, by a student of military as well as naval warfare, to present [15] a reasoned outline of a part of the operations of the war, interspersed with such reflections upon naval warfare, in its generals and its particulars, as have arisen naturally in the course of the story. The method adopted, consequently, is the second of those mentioned in the beginning of these remarks; a consecutive narrative, utilized as a medium for illustrating the principles of war. The application of those principles in this discussion represents the views of one man, believed by him to be in accordance with a considerable body of professional thought, although for this he has no commission to speak; but to some of them also there is, in other quarters, a certain distinct professional opposition.

The aim of the author here, as in all his writings, has been so to present his theme as to invest it with the rational interest attaching to a clear exposition of causes and effects, as shown in a series of events. Where he may have failed, the failure is in himself, not in his subject. The recent Spanish-American War, while possessing, as every war does, characteristics of its own, differentiating it from others, nevertheless, in its broad analogies, falls into [16] line with its predecessors, evidencing that unity of teaching which pervades the art from its beginnings unto this day. It has, moreover, the special value of illustrating the reciprocal needs and offices of the army and the navy, than which no lesson is more valuable to a nation situated as ours is. Protected from any serious attempt at invasion by our isolated position, and by our vast intrinsic strength, we are nevertheless vulnerable in an extensive seaboard, greater, relatively to our population and wealth—great as they are—than that of any other state. Upon this, moreover, rests an immense coasting trade, the importance of which to our internal commercial system is now scarcely realized, but will be keenly felt if we ever are unable to insure its freedom of movement.

We also are committed, inevitably and irrevocably, to an over-sea policy, to the successful maintenance of which will be needed, not only lofty political conceptions of right and of honor, but also the power to support, and if need be to enforce, the course of action which such conceptions shall from time to time demand. Such maintenance will depend [17] primarily upon the navy, but not upon it alone; there will be needed besides an adequate and extremely mobile army, and an efficient correlation of the one with the other, based upon an accurate conception of their respective functions. The true corrective to the natural tendency of each to exaggerate its own importance to the common end is to be found only in some general understanding of the subject diffused throughout the body of the people, who are the ultimate arbiters of national policy.

In short, the people of the United States will need to understand, not only what righteousness dictates, but what power, military and naval, requires, in order duly to assert itself. The disappointment and impatience, now being manifested in too many quarters, over the inevitable protraction of the military situation in the Philippines, indicates a lack of such understanding; for, did it exist, men would not need to be told that even out of the best material, of which we have an abundance, a soldier is not made in a day, nor an army in a season; that when these, the necessary tools, are wanting, or are insufficient in [18] number, the work cannot but lag until they are supplied; in short, that in war, as in every calling, he who wills the end must also understand and will the means. It was the same with the wide-spread panic that swept along our seaboard at the beginning of the late war. So far as it was excusable, it was due to the want of previous preparation; so far as it was unreasonable, it was due to ignorance; but both the want of preparation and the ignorance were the result of the preceding general indifference of the nation to military and naval affairs, an indifference which necessarily had found its reflection in the halting and inadequate provisions made by Congress.

Although changes and additions have been introduced where it has seemed expedient, the author has decided to allow these articles to stand, in the main, substantially as written immediately after the close of hostilities. The opening paragraphs, while less applicable, in their immediate purport, to the present moment, are nevertheless not inappropriate as an explanation of the general tenor of the work itself; and they suggest, moreover, [19] another line of reflection upon the influence, imperceptibly exerted, and passively accepted in men's minds, by the quiet passing of even a single calendar year.

The very lapse of time and subsidence of excitement which tend to insure dispassionate and impartial treatment by the historian, and a juster proportion of impression in spectators, tend also to produce indifference and lethargy in the people at large; whereas in fact the need for sustained interest of a practical character still exists. Intelligent provision for the present and future ought now to succeed to the emotional experiences of the actual war. The reading public has been gorged and surfeited with war literature, a fact which has been only too painfully realized by publishers and editors, who purvey for its appetite and have overstocked the larder. Coincident with this has come an immense wave of national prosperity and consequent business activity, which increasingly engross the attention of men's minds. So far as the mere movement of the imagination, or the stirring of the heart is concerned, this reaction to indifference after excessive agitation was inevitable, [20] and is not in itself unduly to be deplored; but it will be a matter, not merely of lasting regret, but of permanent harm, if the nation again sinks into the general apathy concerning its military and naval necessities which previously existed, and which, as the experience of Great Britain has shown, is unfortunately characteristic of popular representative governments, where present votes are more considered than future emergencies. Not the least striking among the analogies of warfare are the sufferings undergone, and the risks of failure incurred, through imperfect organization, in the Crimea, and in our own recent hostilities with Spain. And let not the public deceive itself, nor lay the fault exclusively, or even chiefly, upon its servants, whether in the military services or in the halls of Congress. The one and the other will respond adequately to any demand made upon them, if the means are placed betimes in their hands; and the officers of the army and navy certainly have not to reproach themselves, as a body, with official failure to represent the dangers, the exposure, and the needs of the commonwealth. It should be needless to add that circumstances [21] now are greatly changed, through the occurrences of last year; and that henceforth the risks from neglect, if continued, will vastly exceed those of former days. The issue lies with the voters.

I ToC

How the Motive of the War gave Direction to its Earlier Movements.—Strategic Value of Puerto Rico.—Considerations on the Size and Qualities of Battleships.—Mutual Relations of Coast Defence and Navy.

It is a common and a true remark that final judgment cannot be passed upon events still recent. Not only is time required for the mere process of collecting data, of assorting and testing the numerous statements, always imperfect and often conflicting, which form the material for history, but a certain and not very short interval must be permitted to elapse during which men's brains and feelings may return to normal conditions, and permit the various incidents which have exalted or depressed them to be seen in their totality, as well as in their true relative importance. There [22] are thus at least two distinct operations essential to that accuracy of judgment to which alone finality can be attributed,—first, the diligent and close study of detail, by which knowledge is completed; and, second, a certain detachment of the mind from the prejudgments and passions engendered by immediate contact, a certain remoteness, corresponding to the idea of physical distance, in virtue of which confusion and distortion of impression disappear, and one is enabled not only to distinguish the decisive outlines of a period, but also to relegate to their true place in the scheme subordinate details which, at the moment of occurrence, had made an exaggerated impression from their very nearness.

It is yet too soon to look for such fulness and justness of treatment in respect to the late hostilities with Spain. Mere literal truth of narrative cannot yet be attained, even in the always limited degree to which historical truth is gradually elicited from a mass of partial and often irreconcilable testimony; and literal truth, when presented, needs to be accompanied by a discriminating analysis and estimate of the influence exerted upon the general result by [23] individual occurrences, positive or negative. I say positive or negative, for we are too apt to overlook the vast importance of negative factors, of inaction as compared to action, of things not done in comparison with those that were done, of mistakes of omission as contrasted with those of commission. Too frequently men, spectators or actors in careers essentially of action, imagine that a safe course is being held because things continue seemingly as they were; whereas, at least in war, failure to dare greatly is often to run the greatest of risks. "Admiral Hotham," wrote Nelson in 1795, "is perfectly satisfied that each month passes without any losses on our side." The result of this purely negative conduct, of this military sin of mere omission, was that Bonaparte's great Italian campaign of 1796 became possible, that the British Fleet was forced to quit the Mediterranean, and the map of Europe was changed. It is, of course, a commonplace that things never really remain as they were; that they are always getting better or worse, at least relatively.

But while it is true that men must perforce be content to wait a while for the full and sure [24] accounts, and for the summing up which shall pass a final judgment upon the importance of events and upon the reputations of the actors in them, it is also true that in the drive of life, and for the practical guidance of life, which, like time and tide, waits for no man, a rapid, and therefore rough, but still a working decision must be formed from the new experiences, and inferences must be drawn for our governance in the present and the near future, whose exigencies attend us. Absolutely correct conclusions, if ever attained in practical life, are reached by a series of approximations; and it will not do to postpone action until exhaustive certainty has been gained. We have tried it at least once in the navy, watching for a finality of results in the experimental progress of European services. What the condition of our own fleet was at the end of those years might be fresh in all our memories, if we had time to remember. Delayed action maybe eminently proper at one moment; at another it may mean the loss of opportunity. Nor is the process of rapid decision—essential in the field—wholly unsafe in council, if inference and conclusion are checked by [25] reference to well-settled principles and fortified by knowledge of the experience of ages upon whose broad bases those principles rest. Pottering over mechanical details doubtless has its place, but it tends to foster a hesitancy of action which wastes time more valuable than the resultant gain.

The preceding remarks indicate sufficiently the scope of these papers. It is not proposed to give a complete story of the operations, for which the material is not yet available. Neither will it be attempted to pronounce decisions absolutely final, for the time is not yet ripe. The effort will be rather to suggest general directions to thought, which may be useful to a reader as he follows the many narratives, official or personal, given to the public; to draw attention to facts and to analogies; to point out experiences, the lessons from which may be profitable in determining the character of the action that must speedily be taken to place the sea power of the Republic upon a proper material basis; and, finally, to bring the course of this war into relation with the teachings of previous history,—the experiences of the recent past to reinforce or to modify those of the [26] remoter past; for under superficial diversity, due to differences of conditions, there often rests fundamental identity, the recognition of which equips the mind, quickens it, and strengthens it for grappling with the problems of the present and the future. The value of history to us is as a record of human experience; but experiences must be understood.

The character and the direction of the first movements of the United States in this conflict with Spain were determined by the occasion, and by the professed object, of the hostilities. As frequently happens, the latter began before any formal declaration of war had been made; and, as the avowed purpose and cause of our action were not primarily redress for grievances of the United States against Spain, but to enforce the departure of the latter from Cuba, it followed logically that the island became the objective of our military movements, as its deliverance from oppression was the object of the war. Had a more general appreciation of the situation been adopted, a view embracing the undeniable injury to the United States, from the then existing conditions, and the generally iniquitous character of Spanish rule in [27] the colonies, and had war for these reasons been declared, the objective of our operations might have been differently chosen for strategic reasons; for our leading object in such case would not have been to help Cuba, but to constrain Spain, and to compel her to such terms as we might demand. It would have been open, for instance, to urge that Puerto Rico, being between five and six hundred miles from the eastern end of Cuba and nearly double that distance from the two ports of the island most important to Spain,—Havana on the north and Cienfuegos on the south,—would be invaluable to the mother country as an intermediate naval station and as a base of supplies and reinforcements for both her fleet and army; that, if left in her undisturbed possession, it would enable her, practically, to enjoy the same advantage of nearness to the great scene of operations that the United States had in virtue of our geographical situation; and that, therefore, the first objective of the war should be the eastern island, and its reduction the first object. The effect of this would have been to throw Spain back upon her home territory for the support of any operations in [28] Cuba, thus entailing upon her an extremely long line of communications, exposed everywhere throughout its course, but especially to the molestation of small cruisers issuing from the harbors of Puerto Rico, which flank the routes, and which, upon the supposition, would have passed into our hands. This view of the matter was urged upon the writer, a few days before hostilities began, by a very old and intelligent naval officer who had served in our own navy and in that of the Confederate States. To a European nation the argument must have been quite decisive; for to it, as distant, or more distant than Spain from Cuba, such an intermediate station would have been an almost insurmountable obstacle while in an enemy's hands, and an equally valuable base if wrested from him. To the United States these considerations were applicable only in part; for, while the inconvenience to Spain would be the same, the gain to us would be but little, as our lines of communication to Cuba neither required the support of Puerto Rico, nor were by it particularly endangered.

This estimate of the military importance of Puerto Rico should never be lost sight of [29] by us as long as we have any responsibility, direct or indirect, for the safety or independence of Cuba. Puerto Rico, considered militarily, is to Cuba, to the future Isthmian canal, and to our Pacific coast, what Malta is, or may be, to Egypt and the beyond; and there is for us the like necessity to hold and strengthen the one, in its entirety and in its immediate surroundings, that there is for Great Britain to hold the other for the security of her position in Egypt, for her use of the Suez Canal, and for the control of the route to India. It would be extremely difficult for a European state to sustain operations in the eastern Mediterranean with a British fleet at Malta. Similarly, it would be very difficult for a transatlantic state to maintain operations in the western Caribbean with a United States fleet based upon Puerto Rico and the adjacent islands. The same reasons prompted Bonaparte to seize Malta in his expedition against Egypt and India in 1798. In his masterly eyes, as in those of Nelson, it was essential to the communications between France, Egypt, and India. His scheme failed, not because Malta was less than invaluable, but for want of adequate [30] naval strength, without which no maritime position possesses value.

There were, therefore, in America two possible objectives for the United States, in case of a war against Spain waged upon grounds at all general in their nature; but to proceed against either was purely a question of relative naval strength. Unless, and until, the United States fleet available for service in the Caribbean Sea was strong enough to control permanently the waters which separated the Spanish islands from our territory nearest to them, the admitted vast superiority of this country in potential resources for land warfare was completely neutralized. If the Spanish Navy preponderated over ours, it would be evidently impossible for transports carrying troops and supplies to traverse the seas safely; and, unless they could so do, operations of war in the enemy's colonies could neither be begun nor continued. If, again, the two fleets were so equally balanced as to make the question of ultimate preponderance doubtful, it was clearly foolish to land in the islands men whom we might be compelled, by an unlucky sea-fight, to abandon there.

[31] This last condition was that which obtained, as war became imminent. The force of the Spanish Navy—on paper, as the expression goes—was so nearly equal to our own that it was well within the limits of possibility that an unlucky incident—the loss, for example, of a battleship—might make the Spaniard decisively superior in nominal, or even in actual, available force. An excellent authority told the writer that he considered that the loss of the *Maine* had changed the balance—that is, that whereas with the *Maine* our fleet had been slightly superior, so after her destruction the advantage, still nominal, was rather the other way. We had, of course, a well-founded confidence in the superior efficiency of our officers and men, and in the probable better condition of our ships and guns; but where so much is at stake as the result of a war, or even as the unnecessary prolongation of war, with its sufferings and anxieties, the only safe rule is to regard the apparent as the actual, until its reality has been tested. However good their information, nations, like fencers, must try their adversary's force before they take liberties. Reconnaissance must precede decisive action. [32] There was, on the part of the Navy Department, no indisposition to take risks, provided success, if obtained, would give an adequate gain. It was clearly recognized that war cannot be made without running risks; but it was also held, unwaveringly, that no merely possible success justified risk, unless it gave a fair promise of diminishing the enemy's naval force, and so of deciding the control of the sea, upon which the issue of the war depended. This single idea, and concentration of purpose upon it, underlay and dictated every step of the Navy Department from first to last,—so far, at least, as the writer knows,—and it must be borne in mind by any reader who wishes to pass intelligent judgment upon the action or non-action of the Department in particular instances.

It was this consideration that brought the *Oregon* from the Pacific to the Atlantic,—a movement initiated before hostilities opened, though not concluded until after they began. The wisdom of the step was justified not merely, nor chiefly, by the fine part played by that ship on July 3, but by the touch of certainty her presence imparted to the grip of our fleet upon Cervera's squadron during the [33] preceding month, and the consequent power to move the army without fear by sea to Santiago. Few realize the doubts, uncertainties, and difficulties of the sustained watchfulness which attends such operations as the "bottling" of the Spanish fleet by Admiral Sampson; for "bottling" a hostile fleet does not resemble the chance and careless shoving of a cork into a half-used bottle,—it is rather like the wiring down of champagne by bonds that cannot be broken and through which nothing can ooze. This it is which constitutes the claim of the American Commander-in-Chief upon the gratitude of his countrymen; for to his skill and tenacity in conducting that operation is primarily due the early ending of the war, the opportunity to remove our stricken soldiery from a sickly climate, the ending of suspense, and the saving of many lives. "The moment Admiral Cervera's fleet was destroyed," truly said the London "Times" (August 16), "the war was practically at an end, unless Spain had elected to fight on to save the point of honor;" for she could have saved nothing else by continued war.

To such successful operation, however, there [34] is needed not only ships individually powerful, but numbers of such ships; and that the numbers of Sampson's fleet were maintained—not drawn off to other, though important, operations—even under such sore temptation as the dash of Cámara's fleet from Cadiz towards the Philippines, was due to the Department's ability to hold fast the primary conception of concentration upon a single purpose, even though running thereby such a risk as was feared from Cámara's armored ships reaching Dewey's unarmored cruisers before they were reinforced. The chances of the race to Manila, between Cámara, when he started from Cadiz, and the two monitors from San Francisco, were deliberately taken, in order to ensure the retention of Cervera's squadron in Santiago, or its destruction in case of attempted escape. Not till that was sufficiently provided for would Watson's division be allowed to depart. Such exclusive tenacity of purpose, under suspense, is more difficult of maintenance than can be readily recognized by those who have not undergone it. To avoid misconception, it should be added here that our division at the Philippines was not itself endangered, although it [35] was quite possible that Manila Bay might have to be temporarily abandoned if Cámara kept on. The movements of the monitors were well in hand, and their junction assured, even under the control of a commander of less conspicuous ability than that already shown by Admiral Dewey. The return of the united force would speedily have ensured Cámara's destruction and the restoration of previous conditions. It is evident, however, that a certain amount of national mortification, and possibly of political complication, might have occurred in the interim.

The necessity and the difficulty of thus watching the squadrons of an enemy within his ports—of "blockading" them, to use a common expression, of "containing" them, to conform to a strictly accurate military terminology—are more familiar to the British naval mind than to ours; for, both by long historical experience and by present-day needs, the vital importance of so narrowly observing the enemy's movements has been forced upon its consciousness. A committee of very distinguished British admirals a few years since reported that, having in view the difficulty of the [36] operation in itself, and the chances of the force detailed falling below its *minimum* by accidents, or by absence for coal or refits, British naval supremacy, vital to the Empire, demanded the number of five British battleships to three of the fleet thus to be controlled. Admiral Sampson's armored ships numbered seven to Cervera's four, a proportion not dissimilar; but those seven were all the armored ships, save monitors, worthless for such purpose, that the United States owned, or would own for some months yet to come. It should be instructive and convincing to the American people to note that when two powerful armored ships of the enemy were thus on their way to attack at one end of the world an admiral and a division that had deserved so well of their country, our whole battle-fleet, properly so called, was employed to maintain off Santiago the proportions which foreign officers, writing long before the conditions arose, had fixed as necessary. Yet the state with which we were at war ranks very low among naval Powers.

The circumstance possesses a furthermost practical present interest, from its bearing upon the question between numbers and individual [37] size in the organization of the naval line of battle; for the ever importunate demand for increase in dimensions in the single ship is already upon the United States Navy, and to it no logical, no simply rational, limit has yet been set This question may be stated as follows: A country can, or will, pay only so much for its war fleet. That amount of money means so much aggregate tonnage. How shall that tonnage be allotted? And, especially, how shall the total tonnage invested in armored ships be divided? Will you have a few very big ships, or more numerous medium ships? Where will you strike your mean between numbers and individual size? You cannot have both, unless your purse is unlimited. The Santiago incident, alike in the battle, in the preceding blockade, and in the concurrent necessity of sending battleships to Dewey, illustrates various phases of the argument in favor of numbers as against extremes of individual size. Heavier ships were not needed; fewer ships might have allowed some enemy to escape; when Cervera came out, the *Massachusetts* was coaling at Guantanamo, and the *New York* necessarily several miles distant, [38] circumstances which, had the ships been bigger and fewer, would have taken much more, proportionately, from the entire squadron at a critical moment. Above all, had that aggregate, 65,934 of tonnage, in seven ships, been divided among five only, of 13,000 each, I know not how the two ships that were designated to go with Watson to the Philippines could possibly have sailed.

The question is momentous, and claims intelligent and immediate decision; for tonnage once locked up in a built ship cannot be got out and redistributed to meet the call of the moment. Neither may men evade a definite conclusion by saying that they will have both unlimited power—that is, size—and unlimited number; for this they cannot have. A decision must be reached, and upon it purpose must be concentrated unwaveringly; the disadvantages as well as the advantages of the choice must be accepted with singleness of mind. Individual size is needed, for specific reasons; numbers also are necessary. Between the two opposing demands there is doubtless a mean of individual size which will ensure the maximum offensive power *of the fleet*; for that, and not the [39] maximum power of the single ship, is the true object of battleship construction. Battleships in all ages are meant to act together, in fleets; not singly, as mere cruisers.

A full discussion of all the considerations, on one side or the other, of this question, would demand more space, and more of technical detail, than the scope of these papers permits. As with most conclusions of a concrete character dealing with contradictory elements, the result reached will inevitably be rather an approximation than an absolute demonstrable certainty; a broad general statement, not a narrow formula. All rules of War, which is not an exact science, but an art, have this characteristic. They do not tell one exactly how to do right, but they give warning when a step is being contemplated which the experience of ages asserts to be wrong. To an instructed mind they cry silently, "Despite all plausible arguments, this one element involved in that which you are thinking to do shows that in it you will go wrong." In the judgment of the writer, two conditions must be primarily considered in determining a class of battleship to which, for the sake of homogeneousness, most [40] of the fleet should conform. Of these two, one must be given in general terms; the other can be stated with more precision. The chief requisite to be kept in view in the battleship is the offensive power of the fleet of which it is a member. The aggregate gun-power of the fleet remaining the same, the increase of its numbers, by limiting the size of the individual ships, tends, up to a certain point, to increase its offensive power; for war depends largely upon combination, and facility of combination increases with numbers. Numbers, therefore, mean increase of offensive power, other things remaining equal. I do not quote in defence of this position Nelson's saying, that "numbers only can annihilate," because in his day experience had determined a certain mean size of working battleship, and he probably meant merely that preponderant numbers of that type were necessary; but weight may justly be laid upon the fact that our forerunners had, under the test of experience, accepted a certain working mean, and had rejected those above and below that mean, save for exceptional uses.

The second requisite to be fulfilled in the battleship is known technically as coal [41] endurance,—ability to steam a certain distance without recoaling, allowing in the calculation a reasonable margin of safety, as in all designs. This standard distance should be the greatest that separates two coaling places, as they exist in the scheme of fortified coaling ports which every naval nation should frame for itself. In our own case, such distance is that from Honolulu to Guam, in the Ladrones,—3,500 miles. The excellent results obtained from our vessels already in commission, embodying as they do the tentative experiences of other countries, as well as the reflective powers of our own designers, make it antecedently probable that 10,000 and 12,000 tons represent the extremes of normal displacement advantageous for the United States battleship. When this limit is exceeded, observation of foreign navies goes to show that the numbers of the fleet will be diminished and its aggregate gun-power not increased,—that is, ships of 15,000 tons actually have little more gun-power than those of 10,000. Both results are deviations from the ideal of the battle-fleet already given. In the United States Navy the tendency to huge ships needs to be particularly watched, for [42] we have a tradition in their favor, inherited from the successes of our heavy frigates in the early years of this century. It must be recalled, therefore, that those ships were meant to act singly, but that long experience has shown that for fleet operations a mean of size gives greater aggregate efficiency, both in force and in precision of manœuvre. In the battleship great speed also is distinctly secondary to offensive power and to coal endurance.

To return from a long digression. Either Cuba or Puerto Rico might, in an ordinary case of war, have been selected as the first objective of the United States operations, with very good reasons for either choice. What the British island Santa Lucia is to Jamaica, what Martinique would be to France, engaged in important hostilities in the Caribbean, that, in measure, Puerto Rico is to Cuba, and was to Spain. To this was due the general and justifiable professional expectation that Cervera's squadron would first make for that point, although the anchorage at San Juan, the principal port, leaves very much to be desired in the point of military security for a fleet,—a fact that will call for [43] close and intelligent attention on the part of the professional advisers of the Navy Department. But, while either of the Spanish islands was thus eligible, it would have been quite out of the question to attempt both at the same time, our navy being only equal to the nominal force of Spain; nor, it should be added, could a decided superiority over the latter have justified operations against both, unless our numbers had sufficed to overbear the whole of the hostile war fleet at both points. To have the greater force and then to divide it, so that the enemy can attack either or both fractions with decisively superior numbers, is the acme of military stupidity; nor is it the less stupid because in practice it has been frequently done. In it has often consisted the vaunted operation of "surrounding an enemy," "bringing him between two fires," and so forth; pompous and troublesome combinations by which a divided force, that could perfectly well move as a whole, starts from two or three widely separated points to converge upon a concentrated enemy, permitting him meanwhile the opportunity, if alert enough, to strike the divisions in detail.

[44] Having this obvious consideration in mind, it is curious now to recall that in the "North American Review," so lately as February, 1897, appeared an article entitled, "Can the United States afford to fight Spain?" by "A Foreign Naval Officer,"—evidently, from internal indications, a Spaniard,—in which occurred this brilliant statement: "For the purposes of an attack upon Spain in the West Indies, the American fleet would necessarily divide itself into two squadrons, one ostensibly destined for Puerto Rico, the other for Cuba. Spain, before attempting to inflict serious damage upon places on the American coast, would certainly try to cut off the connection between the two American squadrons operating in the West Indies, and to attack each separately." The remark illustrates the fool's paradise in which many Spaniards, even naval officers, were living before the war, as is evidenced by articles in their own professional periodicals. To attribute such folly to us was not complimentary; and I own my remarks, upon first reading it, were not complimentary to the writer's professional competency.

All reasons, therefore, combined to direct [45] the first movement of the United States upon Cuba, and upon Cuba alone, leaving Spain in undisputed possession of such advantages as Puerto Rico might give. But Cuba and Puerto Rico, points for attack, were not, unluckily, the only two considerations forced upon the attention of the United States. We have a very long coast-line, and it was notorious that the defences were not so far advanced, judged by modern standards, as to inspire perfect confidence, either in professional men or in the inhabitants. By some of the latter, indeed, were displayed evidences of panic unworthy of men, unmeasured, irreflective, and therefore irrational; due largely, it is to be feared, to that false gospel of peace which preaches it for the physical comfort and ease of mind attendant, and in its argument against war strives to smother righteous indignation or noble ideals by appealing to the fear of loss,—casting the pearls of peace before the swine of self-interest. But a popular outcry, whether well or ill founded, cannot be wholly disregarded by a representative Government; and, outside of the dangers to the coast,—which, in the case of the larger cities at least, were probably [46] exaggerated,—there was certainly an opportunity for an enterprising enemy to embarrass seriously the great coasting trade carried on under our own flag. There was much idle talk, in Spain and elsewhere, about the injury that could be done to United States commerce by scattered cruisers, commerce-destroyers. It was overlooked that our commerce under our own flag is inconsiderable: there were very few American ships abroad to be captured. But the coasting trade, being wholly under our own flag, was, and remains, an extremely vulnerable interest, one the protection of which will make heavy demands upon us in any maritime war. Nor can it be urged that that interest alone will suffer by its own interruption. The bulky cargoes carried by it cannot be transferred to the coastwise railroads without overtaxing the capacities of the latter; all of which means, ultimately, increase of cost and consequent suffering to the consumer, together with serious injury to all related industries dependent upon this traffic.

Under these combined influences the United States Government found itself confronted from the beginning with two objects of military [47] solicitude, widely divergent one from the other, both in geographical position and in method of action; namely, the attack upon Cuba and the protection of its own shores. As the defences did not inspire confidence, the navy had to supplement their weakness, although it is essentially an offensive, and not a defensive, organization. Upon this the enemy counted much at the first. "To defend the Atlantic coasts in case of war," wrote a Spanish lieutenant who had been Naval Attaché in Washington, "the United States will need one squadron to protect the port of New York and another for the Gulf of Mexico. But if the squadron which it now possesses is devoted to the defence of New York (including Long Island Sound), the coasts of the Gulf of Mexico must be entirely abandoned and left at the mercy of blockade and bombardment." Our total force for the order of battle, prior to the arrival of the *Oregon*, was nominally only equal to that of the enemy, and, when divided between the two objects named, the halves were not decisively superior to the single squadron under Cervera,—which also might be reinforced by some of the armored ships then in Spain. [48] The situation, therefore, was one that is not infrequent, but always embarrassing,—a double purpose and a single force, which, although divisible, ought not to be divided.

It is proper here to say, for the remark is both pertinent and most important, that coast defences and naval force are not interchangeable things; neither are they opponents, one of the other, but complementary. The one is stationary, the other mobile; and, however perfect in itself either may be, the other is necessary to its completeness. In different nations the relative consequence of the two may vary. In Great Britain, whose people are fed, and their raw materials obtained, from the outside world, the need for a fleet vastly exceeds that for coast defences. With us, able to live off ourselves, there is more approach to parity. Men may even differ as to which is the more important; but such difference, in this question, which is purely military, is not according to knowledge. In equal amounts, mobile offensive power is always, and under all conditions, more effective to the ends of war than stationary defensive power. Why, then, provide the latter? Because mobile force, [49] whatever shape it take, ships or men, is limited narrowly as to the weight it can bear; whereas stationary force, generally, being tied to the earth, is restricted in the same direction only by the ability of the designer to cope with the conditions. Given a firm foundation, which practically can always be had, and there is no limit to the amount of armor,—mere defensive outfit,—be it wood, stone, bricks, or iron, that you can erect upon it; neither is there any limit to the weight of guns, the offensive element, that the earth can bear; only they will be motionless guns. The power of a steam navy to move is practically unfettered; its ability to carry weight, whether guns or armor, is comparatively very small. Fortifications, on the contrary, have almost unbounded power to bear weight, whereas their power to move is *nil*; which again amounts to saying that, being chained, they can put forth offensive power only at arm's length, as it were. Thus stated, it is seen that these two elements of sea warfare are in the strictest sense complementary, one possessing what the other has not; and that the difference is fundamental, essential, unchangeable,—not accidental or temporary. Given local [50] conditions which are generally to be found, greater power, defensive and offensive, can be established in permanent works than can be brought to the spot by fleets. When, therefore, circumstances permit ships to be squarely pitted against fortifications,—not merely to pass swiftly by them,—it is only because the builders of the shore works have not, for some reason, possibly quite adequate, given them the power to repel attack which they might have had. It will not be asserted that there are no exceptions to this, as to most general rules; but as a broad statement it is almost universally true. "I took the liberty to observe," wrote Nelson at the siege of Calvi, when the commanding general suggested that some vessels might batter the forts, "that the business of laying wood against walls was much altered of late." Precisely what was in his mind when he said "of late" does not appear, but the phrase itself shows that the conditions which induced any momentary equality between ships and forts when brought within range were essentially transient.

As seaports, and all entrances from the sea, are stationary, it follows naturally that the arrangements for their defence also should, as [51] a rule, be permanent and stationary, for as such they are strongest. Indeed, unless stationary, they are apt not to be permanent, as was conclusively shown in the late hostilities, where all the new monitors, six in number, intended for coast defence, were diverted from that object and despatched to distant points; two going to Manila, and stripping the Pacific coast of protection, so far as based upon them. This is one of the essential vices of a system of coast defence dependent upon ships, even when constructed for that purpose; they are always liable to be withdrawn by an emergency, real or fancied. Upon the danger of such diversion to the local security, Nelson insisted, when charged with the guard of the Thames in 1801. The block ships (floating batteries), he directed, were on no account to be moved for any momentary advantage; for it might very well be impossible for them to regain their carefully chosen positions when wanted there. Our naval scheme in past years has been seriously damaged, and now suffers, from two misleading conceptions: one that a navy is for defence primarily, and not for offensive war; the other, consequent mainly upon the first, that the [52] monitor, being stronger defensively than offensively, and of inferior mobility, was the best type of warship. The Civil War, being, so far as the sea was concerned, essentially a coast war, naturally fostered this opinion. The monitor in smooth water is better able to stand up to shore guns than ships are which present a larger target; but, for all that, it is more vulnerable, both above water and below, than shore guns are if these are properly distributed. It is a hybrid, neither able to bear the weight that fortifications do, nor having the mobility of ships; and it is, moreover, a poor gun-platform in a sea-way.

There is no saying of Napoleon's known to the writer more pregnant of the whole art and practice of war than this, "Exclusiveness of purpose is the secret of great successes and of great operations." If, therefore, in maritime war, you wish permanent defences for your coasts, rely exclusively upon stationary works, if the conditions admit, not upon floating batteries which have the weaknesses of ships. If you wish offensive war carried on vigorously upon the seas, rely exclusively upon ships that have the qualities of ships and not of floating [53] batteries. We had in the recent hostilities 26,000 tons of shipping sealed up in monitors, of comparatively recent construction, in the Atlantic and the Pacific. There was not an hour from first to last, I will venture to say, that we would not gladly have exchanged the whole six for two battleships of less aggregate displacement; and that although, from the weakness of the Spanish defences, we were able to hug pretty closely most parts of the Cuban coast. Had the Spanish guns at Santiago kept our fleet at a greater distance, we should have lamented still more bitterly the policy which gave us sluggish monitors for mobile battleships.

II ToC

The Effect of Deficient Coast-Defence upon the Movements of the Navy.— The Military and Naval Conditions of Spain at the Outbreak of the War.

The unsatisfactory condition of the coast defences, whereby the navy lost the support of its complementary factor in the scheme of national sea power, imposed a vicious, though inevitable, change in the initial [54] plan of campaign, which should have been directed in full force against the coast of Cuba. The four newer monitors on the Atlantic coast, if distributed among our principal ports, were not adequate, singly, to resist the attack which was suggested by the possibilities of the case—though remote—and still more by the panic among certain of our citizens. On the other hand, if the four were massed and centrally placed, which is the correct disposition of any mobile force, military or naval, intended to counteract the attack of an enemy whose particular line of approach is as yet uncertain, their sluggishness and defective nautical qualities would make them comparatively inefficient. New York, for instance, is a singularly central and suitable point, relatively to our northern Atlantic seaboard, in which to station a division intended to meet and thwart the plans of a squadron like Cervera's, if directed against our coast ports, in accordance with the fertile imaginations of evil which were the fashion in that hour. Did the enemy appear off either Boston, the Delaware, or the Chesapeake, he could not effect material injury before a division of ships of the *Oregon* class would be upon him; and [55] within the limits named are found the major external commercial interests of the country as well as the ocean approaches along which they travel. But had the monitors been substituted for battleships, not to speak of their greater slowness, their inferiority as steady gun-platforms would have placed them at a serious disadvantage if the enemy were met outside, as he perfectly well might be.

It was probably such considerations as these, though the writer was not privy to them, that determined the division of the battle fleet, and the confiding to the section styled the Flying Squadron the defence of the Atlantic coast for the time being. The monitors were all sent to Key West, where they would be at hand to act against Havana; the narrowness of the field in which that city, Key West, and Matanzas are comprised making their slowness less of a drawback, while the moderate weather which might be expected to prevail would permit their shooting to be less inaccurate. The station of the Flying Squadron in Hampton Roads, though not so central as New York relatively to the more important commercial interests, upon which, if upon any, the Spanish [56] attack might fall, was more central as regards the whole coast; and, above all, was nearer than New York to Havana and to Puerto Rico. The time element also entered the calculations in another way, for a fleet of heavy ships is more certainly able to put to sea at a moment's notice, in all conditions of tide and weather, from the Chesapeake than from New York Bay. In short, the position chosen may be taken to indicate that, in the opinion of the Navy Department and its advisers, Cervera was not likely to attempt a dash at an Atlantic port, and that it was more important to be able to reach the West Indies speedily than to protect New York or Boston,—a conclusion which the writer entirely shared.

The country, however, should not fail to note that the division of the armored fleet into two sections, nearly a thousand miles apart, though probably the best that could be done under all the circumstances of the moment, was contrary to sound practice; and that the conditions which made it necessary should not have existed. Thus, deficient coast protection reacts unfavorably upon the war fleet, which in all its movements should be free from any [57] responsibility for the mere safety of the ports it quits. Under such conditions as then obtained, it might have been possible for Spain to force our entire battle fleet from its offensive undertaking against Cuba, and to relegate it to mere coast defence. Had Cervera's squadron, instead of being despatched alone to the Antilles, been recalled to Spain, as it should have been, and there reinforced by the two armored ships which afterwards went to Suez with Cámara, the approach of this compact body would have compelled our fleet to concentrate; for each of our divisions of three ships—prior to the arrival of the *Oregon*—would have been too weak to hazard an engagement with the enemy's six. When thus concentrated, where should it be placed? Off Havana, or at Hampton Roads? It could not be at both. The answer undoubtedly should be, "Off Havana;" for there it would be guarding the most important part of the enemy's coast, blocking the access to it of the Spanish fleet, and at the same time covering Key West, our naval base of operations. But if the condition of our coast defences at all corresponded to the tremors of our seaport citizens, the [58] Government manifestly would be unable to hold the fleet thus at the front. Had it, on the contrary, been impossible for an enemy's fleet to approach nearer than three miles to our sea-coast without great and evident danger of having ships damaged which could not be replaced, and of wasting ammunition at ranges too long even for bombardments, the Spanish battle fleet would have kept away, and would have pursued its proper object of supporting their campaign in Cuba by driving off our fleet—if it could. It is true that no amount of fortification will secure the coasting trade beyond easy gunshot of the works; but as the enemy's battle fleet could not have devoted itself for long to molesting the coasters—because our fleet would thereby be drawn to the spot—that duty must have devolved upon vessels of another class, against which we also would have provided, and did provide, by the squadron of cruisers under Commodore Howell. In short, proper coast defence, the true and necessary complement of an efficient navy, releases the latter for its proper work,—offensive, upon the open seas, or off the enemy's shores.

ToList
[59] The subject receives further illumination when we consider, in addition to the hypothetical case just discussed,—the approach of six Spanish ships,—the actual conditions at the opening of the campaign. We had chosen Cuba for our objective, had begun our operations, Cervera was on his way across the ocean, and our battle fleet was divided and posted as stated. It was reasonable for us to estimate each division of our ships—one comprising the *New York*, *Iowa*, and *Indiana*, the other the *Brooklyn*, *Massachusetts*, and *Texas*—as able to meet Cervera's four, these being of a class slightly inferior to the best of ours. We might at least flatter ourselves that, to use a frequent phrase of Nelson's, by the time they had soundly beaten one of these groups, they would give us no more trouble for the rest of the year. We could, therefore, with perfect military propriety, have applied the two divisions to separate tasks on the Cuban coast, if our own coast had been adequately fortified.

The advantage—nay, the necessity—of thus distributing our battleships, having only four enemies to fear, will appear from a glance at the map of Cuba. It will there be seen that [60] the island is particularly narrow abreast of Havana, and that from there, for a couple of hundred miles to the eastward, extends the only tolerably developed railroad system, by which the capital is kept in communication with the seaports, on the north coast as far as Sagua la Grande, and on the south with Cienfuegos and Batabano. This narrowness, and the comparative facility of communication indicated by the railroads, enabled Spain, during her occupation, effectually to prevent combined movements between the insurgents in the east and those in the west; a power which Weyler endeavored to increase by the *trocha* system,—a ditch or ditches, with closely supporting works, extending across the island. Individuals, or small parties, might slip by unperceived; but it should have been impossible for any serious co-operation to take place. The coast-wise railroads, again, kept Havana and the country adjacent to them in open, if limited, communication with the sea, so long as any one port upon their lines remained unblockaded. For reasons such as these, in this belt of land, from Havana to Sagua and Cienfuegos, lay the chief strength of the Spanish [61] tenure, which centred upon Havana; and in it the greatest part of the Spanish army was massed. Until, therefore, we were ready to invade, which should not have been before the close of the rainy season, the one obvious course open to us was to isolate the capital and the army from the sea, through which supplies of all kinds—daily bread, almost, of food and ammunition—were introduced; for Cuba, in these respects, produces little.

To perfect such isolation, however, it was necessary not only to place before each port armed cruisers able to stop merchant steamers, but also to give to the vessels so stationed, as well on the south as on the north side, a backbone of support by the presence of an armored fleet, which should both close the great ports—Havana and Cienfuegos—and afford a rallying-point to the smaller ships, if driven in by the appearance of Cervera's division. The main fleet—three armored ships—on the north was thus used, although the blockade, from the fewness of available cruisers, was not at first extended beyond Cardenas. On the south a similar body—the Flying Squadron—should from the first have been stationed [62] before Cienfuegos;

for each division, as has been said, could with military propriety have been risked singly against Cervera's four ships. This was not done, because it was possible—though most improbable—that the Spanish squadron might attempt one of our own ports; because we had not perfect confidence in the harbor defences; and because, also, of the popular outcry. Consequently, the extremely important port of Cienfuegos, a back door to Havana, was blockaded only by a few light cruisers; and when the Spanish squadron was reported at Curaçao, these had to be withdrawn. One only was left to maintain in form the blockade which had been declared; and she had instructions to clear out quickly if the enemy appeared. Neither one, nor a dozen, of such ships would have been the slightest impediment to Cervera's entering Cienfuegos, raising our blockade by force; and this, it is needless to add, would have been hailed in Spain and throughout the Continent of Europe as a distinct defeat for us,—which, in truth, it would have been, carrying with it consequences political as well as military.

This naval mishap, had it occurred, would [63] have been due mainly to inadequate armament of our coasts; for to retain the Flying Squadron in the Chesapeake, merely as a guard to the coasting trade, would have been a serious military error, subordinating an offensive operation—off Cienfuegos—to one merely defensive, and not absolutely vital. "The best protection against an enemy's fire," said Farragut, "is a well-directed fire from our own guns." Analogically, the best defence for one's own shores is to harass and threaten seriously those of the opponent; but this best defence cannot be employed to the utmost, if the inferior, passive defence of fortification has been neglected. The fencer who wears also a breastplate may be looser in his guard. Seaports cannot strike beyond the range of their guns; but if the great commercial ports and naval stations can strike effectively so far, the fleet can launch into the deep rejoicing, knowing that its home interests, behind the buckler of the fixed defences, are safe till it returns.

The broader determining conditions, and the consequent dispositions made by the Government of the United States and its naval authorities, in the recent campaign, have now [64] been stated and discussed. In them is particularly to be noted the crippling effect upon naval operations produced by the consciousness of inadequate coast defences of the permanent type. The sane conclusion to be drawn is, that while sea-coast fortification can never take the place of fleets; that while, as a defence even, it, being passive, is far inferior to the active measure of offensive defence, which protects its own interests by carrying offensive war out on to the sea, and, it may be, to the enemy's shores; nevertheless, by the fearless freedom of movement it permits to the navy, it is to the latter complementary,—completes it; the two words being etymologically equivalent.

The other comments hitherto made upon our initial plan of operations—for example, the impropriety of attempting simultaneous movements against Puerto Rico and Cuba, and the advisability or necessity, under the same conditions, of moving against both Cienfuegos and Havana by the measure of a blockade—were simply special applications of general principles of warfare, universally true, to particular instances in this campaign. They [65] address themselves, it may be said, chiefly to the soldier or seaman, as illustrating his especial business of directing war; and while their value to the civilian cannot be denied,—for whatever really enlightens public opinion in a country like ours facilitates military operations,—nevertheless the function of coast defence, as contributory to sea power, is a lesson most necessary to be absorbed by laymen; for it, as well as the maintenance of the fleet, is in this age the work of peace times, when the need of preparation for war is too little heeded to be understood. The illustrations of the embarrassment actually incurred from this deficiency in the late hostilities are of the nature of an object lesson, and as such should be pondered.

At the same time, however, that attention is thus called to the inevitable and far-reaching effect of such antecedent neglects, shown in directions where men would not ordinarily have expected them, it is necessary to check exaggeration of coast defence, in extent or in degree, by remarking that in any true conception of war, fortification, defence, inland and sea-coast alike, is of value merely in so far as it conduces to offensive operations. This is [66] conspicuously illustrated by our recent experience. The great evil of our deficiencies in coast armament was that they neutralized temporarily a large part of our navy; prevented our sending it to Cuba; made possible that Cervera's squadron, during quite an interval, might do this or that thing of several things thus left open to him, the result of which would have been to encourage the enemy, and possibly to produce political action by our ill-wishers abroad. Directly upon this consideration—of the use that the Flying Squadron might have been, if not held up for coast defence—follows the further reflection how much more useful still would have been a third squadron; that is, a navy half as large again as we then had. Expecting Cervera's force alone, a navy of such size, free from anxiety about coast defence, could have barred to him San Juan de Puerto Rico as well as Cienfuegos and Havana; or had Cámara been joined to Cervera, as he should have been, such a force would have closed both Cienfuegos and Havana with divisions that need not have feared the combined enemy. If, further, there had been a fourth squadron—our coast defence in each case [67] remaining the same—our evident naval supremacy would probably have kept the Spanish fleet in Europe. Not unlikely there would have been no war; in which event, the anti-imperialist may observe there would, thanks to a great and prepared navy, have been no question of the Philippines, and possibly none of Hawaii.

In short, it is with coast defence and the navy as it is with numbers *versus* size in battleships. Both being necessary, the question of proportion demands close attention, but in both cases the same single principle dominates: offensive power, not defensive, determines the issues of war. In the solution of the problem, the extent to be given coast defence by fortification depends, as do all military decisions, whether of preparation or of actual warfare, upon certain well-recognized principles; and for a given country or coast, since the natural conditions remain permanent, the general dispositions, and the relative power of the several works, if determined by men of competent military knowledge, will remain practically constant during long periods. It is true, doubtless, that purely military conclusions [68] must submit to some modification, in deference to the liability of a population to panics. The fact illustrates again the urgent necessity for the spread of sound elementary ideas on military subjects among the people at large; but, if the great coast cities are satisfied of their safety, a government will be able to resist the unreasonable clamor—for such it is—of small towns and villages, which are protected by their own insignificance. The navy is a more variable element; for the demands upon it depend upon external conditions of a political character, which may undergo changes not only sudden, but extensive. The results of the war with Spain, for instance, have affected but little the question of passive coast defence, by fortification or otherwise; but they have greatly altered the circumstances which hitherto have dictated the size of our active forces, both land and sea. Upon the greater or less strength of the navy depends, in a maritime conflict, the aggressive efficiency which shortens war, and so mitigates its evils. In the general question of preparation for naval war, therefore, the important centres and internal waterways of commerce must receive local protection, where they [69] are exposed to attack from the sea; the rest must trust, and can in such case safely trust, to the fleet, upon which, as the offensive arm, all other expenditure for military maritime efficiency should be made. The preposterous and humiliating terrors of the past months, that a hostile fleet would waste coal and ammunition in shelling villages and bathers on a beach, we may hope will not recur.

Before proceeding to study the operations of the war, the military and naval conditions of the enemy at its outbreak must be briefly considered.

Spain, being a state that maintains at all times a regular army, respectable in numbers as well as in personal valor, had at the beginning, and, from the shortness of the war, continued to the end to have a decided land superiority over ourselves. Whatever we might hope eventually to produce in the way of an effective army, large enough for the work in Cuba, time was needed for the result, and time was not allowed. In one respect only the condition of the Peninsula seems to have resembled our own; that was in the inadequacy of the coast defences. The matter there was even more [70] serious than with us, because not only were the preparations less, but several large sea-coast cities—for instance, Barcelona, Malaga, Cadiz—lie immediately upon the seashore; whereas most of ours are at the head of considerable estuaries, remote from the entrance. The exposure of important commercial centres to bombardment, therefore, was for them much greater. This consideration was indeed so evident, that there was in the United States Navy a perceptible current of feeling in favor of carrying maritime war to the coast of Spain, and to its commercial approaches.

The objection to this, on the part of the Navy Department, was, with slight modifications, the same as to the undertaking of operations against Puerto Rico. There was not at our disposition, either in armored ships or in cruisers, any superfluity of force over and above the requirements of the projected blockade of Cuba. To divert ships from this object, therefore, would be false to the golden rule of concentration of effort,—to the single eye that gives light in warfare. Moreover, in such a movement, the reliance, as represented in the writer's hearing, would have been upon [71] moral effect, upon the dismay of the enemy; for we should soon have come to the end of our physical coercion. As Nelson said of bombarding Copenhagen, "We should have done our worst, and no nearer friends." The influence of moral effect in war is indisputable, and often tremendous; but like some drugs in the pharmacopœia, it is very uncertain in its action. The other party may not, as the boys say, "scare worth a cent;" whereas material forces can be closely measured beforehand, and their results reasonably predicted. This statement, generally true, is historically especially true of the Spaniard, attacked in his own land. The tenacity of the race has never come out so strongly as under such conditions, as was witnessed in the old War of the Spanish Succession, and during the usurpation of Napoleon.

On the other hand, such an enterprise on our part, if directed against Spanish commerce on the seas, as was suggested by several excellent officers, would have had but a trivial objective. The commerce of Spain was cut up, root and branch, by our expeditions against her colonies, Cuba and Manila; for her most [72] important trade depended upon monopoly of the colonial markets. The slight stream of traffic maintained in Spanish bottoms between the English Channel and the Peninsula, was so small that it could readily have been transferred to neutral ships, whose flag we had for this war engaged should protect enemy's goods. Under these circumstances, the coasts of the Philippines and of Cuba were to us the coast of Spain, and far more conveniently so than that of the home country would have been. A Spanish merchant captain, writing from Barcelona as early as the 7th of May, had said: "At this moment we have shut up in this port the [steam] fleets of five transatlantic companies," which he names. "The sailing-vessels are tied up permanently. Several [named] ships have fallen into the hands of the enemy. Meantime the blockade of Cuba, Puerto Rico, and Manila continues, at least for our flag, and maritime commerce is at a standstill. In Barcelona some foreign firms, exporters to the Philippines, have failed, as well as several custom-house brokers, owing to the total cessation of mercantile movement. The losses already suffered by our trade are incalculable, [73] amounting to much more than the millions needed to maintain a half-dozen armored ships, which would have prevented the Yankees from daring so much." These vessels continued to lie idle in Barcelona until the dread of Commodore Watson's threatened approach caused them to be sent to Marseilles, seeking the protection of the neutral port. A few weeks later the same Spanish writer comments: "The result of our mistakes," in the management of the navy, "is the loss of the markets of Cuba, Puerto Rico, and the Philippines, and, in consequence, the death of our merchant marine." Inquiries were addressed by the state to the Chambers of Commerce, for suggestions as to the opening of new markets, to compensate for the existing suspension of communications with "the over-sea provinces."

With such results from our operations in the Antilles and the Philippines, there was no inducement, and indeed no justification, for sending cruisers across the ocean, until we had enough and to spare for the blockade of Cuba and Puerto Rico. This was at no time the case, up to the close of the war, owing to a combination of causes. The work of paralyzing Spanish [74] trade was being effectually done by the same measures that tended to strangle the Spanish armies in Cuba and the Philippines, and which, when fully developed, would entirely sever their necessary communications with the outside world. Besides all this, the concentration of our efforts upon Cuba, with a subsequent slight extension to the single port of San Juan in Puerto Rico, imposed upon Spain the burden of sustaining the war between three and four thousand miles from home, and spared us the like additional strain. Every consideration so far entertained, therefore, of energy as well as of prudence, dictated the application of all the pressure at our disposal at the beginning of hostilities, and until the destruction of Cervera's squadron, upon Cuba, and in a very minor degree upon Puerto Rico. Indeed, the ships placed before San Juan were not for blockade, properly so called, but to check any mischievous display of energy by the torpedo cruiser within.

After thus noting briefly the conditions of the enemy's coast defences and commerce, there remains to consider the one other element of his sea power—the combatant navy—with [75] regard to its force and to its disposition when war began.

As was before said, the disparity between the armored fleets of the two nations was nominally inconsiderable; and the Spaniards possessed one extremely valuable—and by us unrivalled—advantage in a nearly homogeneous group of five [1] armored cruisers, very fast, and very similar both in nautical qualities and in armament. It is difficult to estimate too highly the possibilities open to such a body of ships, regarded as a "fleet in being," to use an expression that many of our readers may have seen, but perhaps scarcely fully understood.

The phrase "fleet in being," having within recent years gained much currency in naval writing, demands—like the word "jingo"—preciseness of definition; and this, in general acceptance, it has not yet attained. It remains, therefore, somewhat vague, and so occasions misunderstandings between men whose opinions perhaps do not materially differ. The writer will not attempt to define, but a brief [76] explanation of the term and its origin may not be amiss. It was first used, in 1690, by the British admiral Lord Torrington, when defending his course in declining to engage decisively, with an inferior force, a French fleet, then dominating in the Channel, and under cover of which it was expected that a descent upon the English coast would be made by a great French army. "Had I fought otherwise," he said, "our fleet had been totally lost, and the kingdom had lain open to invasion. As it was, most men were in fear that the French would invade; but I was always of another opinion, for I always said that whilst we had a fleet in being, they would not dare to make an attempt."

A "fleet in being," therefore, is one the existence and maintenance of which, although inferior, on or near the scene of operations, is a perpetual menace to the various more or less exposed interests of the enemy, who cannot tell when a blow may fall, and who is therefore compelled to restrict his operations, otherwise possible, until that fleet can be destroyed or neutralized. It corresponds very closely to "a position on the flank and rear" of an enemy, [77] where the presence of a smaller force, as every military student knows, harasses, and may even paralyze offensive movements. When such a force is extremely mobile, as a fleet of armored cruisers may be, its power of mischief is very great; potentially, it is forever on the flank and rear, threatening the lines of communications. It is indeed as a threat to communications that the "fleet in being" is chiefly formidable.

The theory received concrete and convincing illustration during the recent hostilities, from the effect exerted—and justly exerted—upon our plans and movements by Cervera's squadron, until there had been assembled before Santiago a force at once so strong and so numerous as to make his escape very improbable. Even so, when a telegram was received from a capable officer that he had identified by night, off the north coast of Cuba, an armored cruiser,—which, if of that class, was most probably an enemy,—the sailing of Shafter's expedition was stopped until the report could be verified. So much for the positive, material influence—in the judgment of the writer, the reasonable influence—of a "fleet in being." As regards the moral effect, the effect upon the [78] imagination, it is scarcely necessary more than to allude to the extraordinary play of the fancy, the kaleidoscopic effects elicited from our own people, and from some foreign critics, in propounding dangers for ourselves and ubiquity for Cervera. Against the infection of such tremors it is one of the tasks of those in responsibility to guard themselves and, if possible, their people. "Don't make pictures for yourself," was Napoleon's warning to his generals. "Every naval operation since

I became head of the government has failed, because my admirals see double and have learned—where I don't know—that war can be made without running risks."

The probable value of a "fleet in being" has, in the opinion of the writer, been much overstated; for, even at the best, the game of evasion, which this is, if persisted in, can have but one issue. The superior force will in the end run the inferior to earth. In the meanwhile, however, vital time may have been lost. It is conceivable, for instance, that Cervera's squadron, if thoroughly effective, might, by swift and well-concealed movements, have detained our fleet in the West Indies [79] until the hurricane of September, 1898, swept over the Caribbean. We had then no reserve to replace armored ships lost or damaged. But, for such persistence of action, there is needed in each unit of the "fleet in being" an efficiency rarely attainable, and liable to be lost by unforeseen accident at a critical moment. Where effect, nay, safety, depends upon mere celerity of movement, as in retreat, a crippled ship means a lost ship; or a lost fleet, if the body sticks to its disabled member. Such efficiency it is probable Cervera's division never possessed. The length of its passage across the Atlantic, however increased by the embarrassment of frequently recoaling the torpedo destroyers, so far over-passed the extreme calculations of our naval authorities, that ready credence was given to an apparently authentic report that it had returned to Spain; the more so that such concentration was strategically correct, and it was incorrect to adventure an important detachment so far from home, without the reinforcement it might have received in Cadiz. This delay, in ships whose individual speed had originally been very high, has been [80] commonly attributed in our service to the inefficiency of the engine-room force; and this opinion is confirmed by a Spanish officer writing in their "Revista de la Marina." "The Americans," he says, "keep their ships cruising constantly, in every sea, and therefore have a large and qualified engine-room force. We have but few machinists, and are almost destitute of firemen." This inequality, however, is fundamentally due to the essential differences of mechanical capacity and development in the two nations. An amusing story was told the writer some years ago by one of our consuls in Cuba. Making a rather rough passage between two ports, he saw an elderly Cuban or Spanish gentleman peering frequently into the engine-room, with evident uneasiness. When asked the cause of his concern, the reply was, "I don't feel comfortable unless the man in charge of the engines talks English to them."

When to the need of constant and sustained ability to move at high speed is added the necessity of frequent recoaling, allowing the hostile navy time to come up, it is evident that the active use of a "fleet in being," however [81] perplexing to the enemy, must be both anxious and precarious to its own commander. The contest is one of strategic wits, and it is quite possible that the stronger, though slower, force, centrally placed, may, in these days of cables, be able to receive word and to corner its antagonist before the latter can fill his bunkers. Of this fact we should probably have received a very convincing illustration, had a satisfactory condition of our coast defences permitted the Flying Squadron to be off Cienfuegos, or even off Havana, instead of in Hampton Roads. Cervera's entrance to Santiago was known to us within twenty-four hours. In twenty-four more it could have been communicated off Cienfuegos by a fast despatch boat, after which less than forty-eight would have placed our division before Santiago. The uncertainty felt by Commodore Schley, when he arrived off Cienfuegos, as to whether the Spanish division was inside or no, would not have existed had his squadron been previously blockading; and his consequent delay of over forty-eight hours—with the rare chance thus offered to Cervera—would not have occurred. To coal four great ships within that time was [82] probably beyond the resources of Santiago; whereas the speed predicated for our own movements is rather below than above the dispositions contemplated to ensure it.

The great end of a war fleet, however, is not to chase, nor to fly, but to control the seas. Had Cervera escaped our pursuit at Santiago, it would have been only to be again paralyzed at Cienfuegos or at Havana. When speed, not force, is the reliance, destruction may be postponed, but can be escaped only by remaining in port. Let it not, therefore, be inferred, from the possible, though temporary, effect of a "fleet in being," that speed is the chief of all factors in the battleship. This plausible, superficial notion, too easily accepted in these days of hurry and of unreflecting dependence upon machinery as the all in all, threatens much harm to the future efficiency of the navy. Not speed, but power of offensive action, is the dominant factor in war. The decisive preponderant element of great land forces has ever been the infantry, which, it is needless to say, is also the slowest. The homely summary of the art of war, "To get there first with the most men," has with strange perverseness been so [83] distorted in naval—and still more in popular—conception, that the second and more important consideration has been subordinated to the former and less essential. Force does not exist for mobility, but mobility for force. It is of no use to get there first unless, when the enemy in turn arrives, you have also the most men,—the greater force. This is especially true of the sea, because there inferiority of force—of gun power—cannot be compensated, as on land it at times may be, by judiciously using accidents of the ground. I do not propose to fall into an absurdity of my own by questioning the usefulness of higher speed, *provided* the increase is not purchased at the expense of strictly offensive power; but the time has come to say plainly that its value is being exaggerated; that it is in the battleship secondary to gun power; that a battle fleet can never attain, nor maintain, the highest rate of any ship in it, except of that one which at the moment is the slowest, for it is a commonplace of naval action that fleet speed is that of the slowest ship; that not exaggerated speed, but uniform speed—sustained speed—is the requisite of the battle fleet; that it is not machinery, as is [84] often affirmed, but brains and guns, that win battles and control the sea. The true speed of war is not headlong precipitancy, but the unremitting energy which wastes no time.

For the reasons that have been given, the safest, though not the most effective, disposition of an inferior "fleet in being" is to lock it up in an impregnable port or ports, imposing upon the enemy the intense and continuous strain of watchfulness against escape. This it was that Torrington, the author of the phrase, proposed for the time to do. Thus it was that Napoleon, to some extent before Trafalgar, but afterward with set and exclusive purpose, used the French Navy, which he was continually augmenting, and yet never, to the end of his reign, permitted again to undertake any serious expedition. The mere maintenance of several formidable detachments, in apparent readiness, from the Scheldt round to Toulon, presented to the British so many possibilities of mischief that they were compelled to keep constantly before each of the French ports a force superior to that within, entailing an expense and an anxiety by which the Emperor hoped to exhaust their endurance. To some extent this [85] was Cervera's position and function in Santiago, whence followed logically the advisability of a land attack upon the port, to force to a decisive issue a situation which was endurable only if incurable. "The destruction of Cervera's squadron," justly commented an Italian writer, before the result was known, "is the only really decisive fact that can result from the expedition to Santiago, because it will reduce to impotence the naval power of Spain. The determination of the conflict will depend throughout upon the destruction of the Spanish sea power, and not upon territorial descents, although the latter may aggravate the situation." The American admiral from before Santiago, when urging the expedition of a land force to make the bay untenable, telegraphed, "The destruction of this squadron will end the war;" and it did.

In other respects it is probable that the Spanish admiral had little confidence in a squadron which, whatever the courage or other qualities of the officers and seamen, had never manœuvred together until it left the Cape de Verde Islands. Since its destruction, a writer in a Spanish naval magazine has told the [86] following incident: "A little more than a year ago we visited General Cervera in La Carraca, [the Cadiz arsenal], and we said to him: 'You appear to be indicated, by professional opinion, for the command of the squadron in case war is declared.' 'In that case,' he replied, 'I shall accept, knowing, however, that I am going to a Trafalgar.' 'And how could that disaster be avoided?' 'By allowing me to expend beforehand fifty thousand tons of coal in evolutions and ten thousand projectiles in target practice. Otherwise we shall go to a Trafalgar. Remember what I say.'"

It is curious to contrast with this well-founded fear of an experienced and gallant officer, expressed in private conversation, the opinion of another Spanish officer, lately Minister of Marine, reported to the Madrid public through a newspaper,—the "Heraldo," of April 6, 1898. It illustrates, further, the curious illusions entertained in high quarters in Spain:

"We had an opportunity to-day of talking for a long time with General Beranger, the last Secretary of the Navy under the Conservative Cabinet. To the questions which we directed [87] to him concerning the conflict pending with the United States, he was kind enough to inform us that he confided absolutely in the triumph of our naval forces. 'We shall conquer on the sea, and I am now going to give you my reasons. The first of these is the remarkable discipline that prevails on our warships; and the second, as soon as fire is opened, the crews of the American ships will commence to desert, since we all know that among them are people of all nationalities. Ship against ship, therefore, a failure is not to be feared. I believe that the squadron detained at Cape de Verde, and particularly the destroyers, should have, and could have, continued the voyage to Cuba, since they have nothing to fear from the American fleet.'"

The review from which Cervera's opinion is quoted has, since the disasters to the Spanish Navy, been full of complaints and of detailed statements concerning the neglect of the navy, both in its material and in drills, during the antecedent months of peace, owing to the practice of a misplaced, if necessary, economy. But that economy, it is justly argued, would not have been required to a disabling degree, [88] if so disproportionate an amount of money had not been expended upon the army, by a state whose great colonial system could in war be sustained only by a fleet. "In more than a year," writes a captain in the Spanish Navy, "we have had only one target practice, and that limited in extent, in order to expend the least possible amount of ammunition." The short brilliant moments of triumph in war are the sign and the seal of the long hours of obscure preparations, of which target practice is but one item. Had even the nominal force of Spain been kept in efficient condition for immediate action, the task of the United States would have been greatly prolonged and far from so easy as it has been since declared by those among our people who delight to belittle the great work our country has just achieved, and to undervalue the magnanimity of its resolution to put a stop to outrages at our doors which were well said to have become intolerable. Neither by land nor by sea was the state of the case so judged by professional men, either at home or abroad. It was indeed evident that, if we persevered, there could be but one issue; but this might have [89] been postponed, by an active opponent, long enough to have disheartened our nation, if it was as easily to be discouraged by the difficulties and dangers, now past, as it is in some quarters represented again to be by the problems arising out of the war and its conquests. Such discouragement, perplexity, and consequent frustration of the adversary's purposes are indeed the prime function of a "fleet in being,"—

to create and to maintain moral effect, in short, rather than physical, unless indeed the enemy, yielding to moral effect, divides his forces in such wise as to give a chance for a blow at one portion of them. The tendency to this also received illustration in our war. "Our seacoast," said a person then in authority to the present writer, "was in a condition of unreasoning panic, and fought to have little squadrons scattered along it everywhere, according to the theory of defence always favored by stupid terror." The "stupidity," by all military experience, was absolute—unqualified; but the Navy Department succeeded in withstanding the "terror"—the moral effect—so far as to compromise on the Flying Squadron; a rational solution, though [90] not unimpeachable. We thus, instead of a half-dozen naval groups, had only two, the combination of which might perhaps be effected in time enough.

FOOTNOTES:

[1] In this number is included the *Emperador Carlos V.*; which, however, did not accompany the other four under Cervera.

III ToC

Possibilities Open To the Spanish Navy at the Beginning of the War.—The Reasons for Blockading Cuba.—First Movements of the Squadrons under Admirals Sampson and Cervera.

For the reasons just stated, it was upon Cervera's squadron that the attention of instructed military students was chiefly turned at the outset of the war. Grave suspicions as to its efficiency, indeed, were felt in many quarters, based partly upon actual knowledge of the neglect of the navy practised by the Spanish Government, and partly upon the inference that the general incapacity evident for years past in all the actions of the Spanish authorities, and notably in Cuba, could not but extend to the navy,—one of the most sensitive and delicate parts of any political organization; one of the first to go to pieces when the social and political foundations of a State are shaken, [91] as was notably shown in the French Revolution. But, though suspected, the ineffectiveness of that squadron could not be assumed before proved. Until then—to use the words of an Italian writer who has treated the whole subject of this war with comprehensive and instructive perspicacity—Spain had "the possibility of contesting the command of the sea, and even of securing a definite preponderance, by means of a squadron possessed of truly exceptional characteristics, both tactical and strategic,"—in short, by means of a "fleet in being."

It is true that in this estimate the writer quoted included the *Carlos V.*, a new and high-powered armored cruiser, and also a number of protected cruisers and of torpedo vessels, of various kinds, all possessing a rate of speed much superior to the more distinctly fighting ships in which consisted the strength of the United States squadrons. Such a fleet, homogeneous in respect to the particular function which constitutes the power of a "fleet in being," whose effectiveness lies in its legs and in its moral effect, in its power to evade pursuit and to play upon the fears of an enemy, should be capable of rapid continuous movement; and [92] such a fleet Spain actually possessed when the war broke out—only it was not ready. "This splendid fleet," resumed our Italian critic, giving rein, perhaps, to a Southern imagination, but not wholly without just reason, "would be in a condition to impose upon the enemy the character which the conflict should assume, alike in strategy and in tactics, and thereby could draw the best and greatest advantage from the actual situation, with a strong probability of partial results calculated to restore the equilibrium between the two belligerent fleets, or even of successes so decisive, if obtained immediately after the declaration of war, as to include a possibility of a Spanish preponderance." The present writer guards himself from being understood to accept fully this extensive programme for a fleet distinctly inferior in actual combative force; but the general assumption of the author quoted indicates the direction of effort which alone held out a hope of success, and which for that reason should have been vigorously followed by the Spanish authorities.

As the Spanish Navy—whatever its defects in organization and practice—is not lacking in [93] thoughtful and instructed officers, it is probable that the despatch of Cervera with only four ships, instead of at least the five armored cruisers well qualified to act together, which he might have had, not to speak of the important auxiliaries also disposable, was due to uninstructed popular and political pressure, of the same kind that in our country sought to force the division of our fleet among our ports. That the Spanish Government was thus goaded and taunted, at the critical period when Cervera was lying in Santiago, is certain. To that, most probably, judging from the words used in the Cortes, we owe the desperate sortie which delivered him into our hands and reduced Spain to inevitable submission. "The continuance of Cervera's division in Santiago, and its apparent inactivity," stated a leading naval periodical in Madrid, issued two days before the destruction of the squadron, "is causing marked currents of pessimism, and of disaffection towards the navy, especially since the Yankees have succeeded in effecting their proposed landing. This state of public feeling, which has been expressed with unrestricted openness in some journals, has been sanctioned [94] in Congress by one of the Opposition members uttering very unguarded opinions, and reflecting injuriously upon the navy itself, as though upon it depended having more or fewer ships." The Minister of Marine, replying in the Cortes, paraphrased as follows, without contradiction, the words of this critic, which voiced, as it would appear, a popular clamor: "You ask, 'Why, after reaching Santiago, has the squadron not gone out, and why does it not now go out?' Why do four ships not go out to fight twenty? You ask again: 'If it does not go out, if it does not hasten to seek death, what is the use of squadrons? For what are fleets built, if not to be lost?' We are bound to believe, Señor Romero Robledo, that your words in this case express neither what you intended to say nor your real opinion." Nevertheless, they seem not to have received correction, nor to have been retracted; and to the sting of them, and of others of like character, is doubtless due the express order of the Ministry under which Cervera quitted his anchorage.

Like ourselves, our enemy at the outset of the war had his fleet in two principal divisions: one still somewhat formless and as yet [95] unready, but of very considerable power, was in the ports of the Peninsula; the other—Cervera's—at the Cape Verde Islands, a possession of Portugal. The latter was really exceptional in its qualities, as our Italian author has said. It was exceptional in a general sense, because homogeneous and composed of vessels of very high qualities, offensive and defensive; it was exceptional also, as towards us in particular, because we had of the same class but two ships,—one-half its own force,—the *New York* and the *Brooklyn*; and, moreover, we had no torpedo cruisers to oppose to the three which accompanied it. These small vessels, while undoubtedly an encumbrance to a fleet in extended strategic movements in boisterous seas, because they cannot always keep up, are a formidable adjunct—tactical in character—in the day of battle, especially if the enemy has none of them; and in the mild Caribbean it was possible that they might not greatly delay their heavy consorts in passages which would usually be short.

The two main divisions of the Spanish fleet were thus about fifteen hundred miles apart when war began on the 25th of April. The [96] neutrality of Portugal made it impossible for Cervera to remain long in his then anchorage, and an immediate decision was forced upon his Government. It is incredible that among the advisers of the Minister of Marine—himself a naval officer—there was no one to point out that to send Cervera at once to the Antilles, no matter to what port, was to make it possible for the United States to prevent any future junction between himself and the remaining vessels of their navy. The squadron of either Sampson or Schley was able to fight him on terms of reasonable equality, to say the least. Either of our divisions, therefore, was capable of blockading him, if caught in port; and it was no more than just to us to infer that, when once thus cornered, we should, as we actually did at Santiago, assemble both divisions, so as to render escape most improbable and the junction of a reinforcement practically impossible. Such, in fact, was the intention from the very first: for, this done, all our other undertakings, Cuban blockade and what not, would be carried on safely, under cover of our watching fleet, were the latter distant ten miles or a thousand from such other operations. The [97] writer, personally, attaches but little importance to the actual consequences of strictly offensive operations attempted by a "fleet in being," when of so inferior force. As suggested by Spanish and foreign officers, in various publications, they have appeared to him fantastic pranks of the imagination, such as he himself indulged in as a boy, rather than a sober judgment formed after considering both sides of the case. "I cannot but admire Captain Owen's zeal," wrote Nelson on one occasion, "in his anxious desire to get at the enemy, but I am afraid it has made him overleap sandbanks and tides, and laid him aboard the enemy. I am as little used to find out the impossible as most folks, and I think I can discriminate between the impracticable and the fair prospect of success." The potentialities of Cervera's squadron, after reaching the Spanish Antilles, must be considered under the limitations of his sandbanks and tides; of telegraph cables betraying his secrets, of difficulties and delays in coaling, of the chances of sudden occasional accidents to which all machinery is liable, multiplied in a fleet by the number of vessels composing it; and to these troubles, inevitable [98] accompaniments of such operations, must in fairness be added the assumption of reasonable watchfulness and intelligence on the part of the United States, in the distribution of its lookouts and of its ships.

The obvious palliative to the disadvantage thus incurred by Spain would have been to add to Cervera ships sufficient to force us at least to unite our two divisions, and to keep them joined. This, however, could not be done at once, because the contingent in Spain was not yet ready; and fear of political consequences and public criticism at home, such as that already quoted, probably deterred the enemy from the correct military measure of drawing Cervera's squadron back to the Canaries, some eight hundred or nine hundred miles; or even to Spain, if necessary. This squadron itself had recently been formed in just this way; two ships being drawn back from the Antilles and two sent forward from the Peninsula. If Spain decided to carry on the naval war in the Caribbean,—and to decide otherwise was to abandon Cuba in accordance with our demand,—she should have sent all the armored ships she could get together, and have [99] thrown herself frankly, and at whatever cost, upon a mere defensive policy for her home waters, relying upon coast defences—or upon mere luck, if need were—for the safety of the ports. War cannot be made without running risks. When you have chosen your field for fighting, you must concentrate upon it, letting your other interests take their chance. To do this, however, men must have convictions, and conviction must rest upon knowledge, or else ignorant clamor and contagious panic will sweep away every reasonable teaching of military experience. And so Cervera went forth with his four gallant ships, foredoomed to his fate by folly, or by national false pride, exhibited in the form of political pressure disregarding sound professional judgment and military experience. We were not without manifestations here of the same uninstructed and ignoble outcry; but fortunately our home conditions permitted it to be disregarded without difficulty. Nevertheless, although under circumstances thus favorable we escaped the worst effects of such lack of understanding, the indications were sufficient to show how hard, in a moment of real emergency, it will be for the Government to [100] adhere to sound military principles, if there be not some appreciation of these in the mass of the people; or, at the very least, among the leaders to whom the various parts of the country are accustomed to look for guidance.

It may be profitable at this point to recall a few dates; after which the narrative, avoiding superfluous details, can be continued in such outline as is required for profitable comment, and for eliciting the more influential factors in the course of events, with the consequent military lessons from them to be deduced.

On April 20th the President of the United States approved the joint resolution passed by the two Houses of Congress, declaring the independence of Cuba, and demanding that Spain should relinquish her authority there and withdraw her forces. A blockade, dated April 22nd, was declared of the north coast of Cuba, from Cardenas on the east to Bahia Honda, west of Havana, and of the port of Cienfuegos on the south side of the island. On April 25th a bill declaring that war between the United States and Spain existed, and had existed since the 21st of the month, was passed by Congress and approved [101] the same evening by the President, thus adding another instance to the now commonplace observation that hostilities more frequently precede than follow a formal declaration. On April 29th, Admiral Cervera's division—four armored cruisers and three torpedo destroyers—quitted the Cape de Verde Islands for an unknown destination, and disappeared during near a fortnight from the knowledge of the United States authorities. On May 1, Commodore Dewey by a dash, the rapidity and audacity of which reflected the highest credit upon his professional qualities, destroyed the Spanish squadron at Manila, thereby paralyzing also all Spanish operations in the East. The Government of the United States was thus, during an appreciable time, and as it turned out finally, released from all military anxiety about the course of events in that quarter.

Meantime the blockade of the Cuban coasts, as indicated above, had been established effectively, to the extent demanded by international law, which requires the presence upon the coast, or before the port, declared blockaded, of such a force as shall constitute a manifest [102] danger of capture to vessels seeking to enter or to depart. In the reserved, not to say unfriendly, attitude assumed by many of the European States, the precise character of which is not fully known, and perhaps never will be, it was not only right, but practically necessary, to limit the extent of coast barred to merchant ships to that which could be thus effectually guarded, leaving to neutral governments no sound ground for complaint. Blockade is one of the rights conceded to belligerent States, by universal agreement, which directly, as well as indirectly, injures neutrals, imposing pecuniary losses by restraints upon trade previously in their hands. The ravages of the insurrection and the narrow policy of Spain in seeking to monopolize intercourse with her colonies had, indeed, already grievously reduced the commerce of the island; but with our war there was sure to spring up a vigorous effort, both legal and contraband, to introduce stores of all kinds, especially the essentials of life, the supply of which was deficient. Such cargoes, not being clearly contraband, could be certainly excluded only by blockade; and the latter, in order fully to [103] serve our military objects, needed at the least to cover every port In railway communication with Havana, where the bulk of the Spanish army was assembled. This it was impossible to effect at the first, because we had not ships enough; and therefore, as always in such cases, a brisk neutral trade, starting from Jamaica and from Mexico, as well as from Europe and the North American Continent, was directed upon the harbors just outside the limits of the blockade,—towards Sagua la Grande and adjacent waters in the north, and to Batabano and other ports in the south.

Such trade would be strictly lawful, from an international standpoint, unless declared by us to be contraband, because aiding to support the army of the enemy; and such declarations, by which provisions are included in the elastic, but ill-defined category of contraband, tend always to provoke the recriminations and unfriendliness of neutral states. Blockade avoids the necessity for definitions, for by it all goods become contraband; the extension of it therefore was to us imperative.

As things were, although this neutral trade frustrated our purposes to a considerable [104] degree, it afforded us no ground for complaint. On the contrary, we were at times hard driven by want of vessels to avoid laying ourselves open to reclamation, on the score of the blockade being invalid, even within its limited range, because ineffective. This was especially the case at the moment when the army was being convoyed from Tampa, as well as immediately before, and for some days after that occasion: before, because it was necessary then to detach from the blockade and to assemble elsewhere the numerous small vessels needed to check the possible harmful activity of the Spanish gunboats along the northern coast, and afterwards, because the preliminary operations about Santiago, concurring with dark nights favorable to Cervera's escape, made it expedient to retain there many of the lighter cruisers, which, moreover, needed recoaling,—a slow business when so many ships were involved. Our operations throughout labored—sometimes more, sometimes less—under this embarrassment, which should be borne in mind as a constant, necessary, yet perplexing element in the naval and military plans. The blockade, in fact, while the army [105] was still unready, and until the Spanish Navy came within reach, was the one decisive measure, sure though slow in its working, which could be taken; the necessary effect of which was to bring the enemy's ships to this side of the ocean, unless Spain was prepared to abandon the contest. The Italian writer already quoted, a fair critic, though Spanish in his leanings, enumerates among the circumstances most creditable to the direction of the war by the Navy Department the perception that "blockade must inevitably cause collapse, given the conditions of insurrection and of exhaustion already existing in the island."

From this specific instance, the same author, whose military judgments show much breadth of view, later on draws a general conclusion which is well worth the attention of American readers, because much of our public thought is committed to the belief that at sea private property, so called,—that is, merchant ships and their cargoes,—should not be liable to capture in war; which, duly interpreted, means that the commerce of one belligerent is not to be attacked or interrupted by the other. "Blockade," says our Italian, "is the [106] fundamental basis of the conflict for the dominion of the seas, when the contest cannot be brought to an immediate issue;" that is, to immediate battle. Blockade, however, is but one form of the unbloody pressure brought to bear upon an enemy by interruption of his commerce. The stoppage of commerce, in whole or in part, exhausts without fighting. It compels peace without sacrificing life. It is the most scientific warfare, because the least sanguinary, and because, like the highest strategy, it is directed against the communications,—the resources,—not the persons, of the enemy. It has been the glory of sea-power that its ends are attained by draining men of their dollars instead of their blood. Eliminate the attack upon an enemy's sea-borne commerce from the conditions of naval war,—in which heretofore it has been always a most important factor,—and the sacrifice of life will be proportionately increased, for two reasons: First, the whole decision of the contest will rest upon actual conflict; and, second, failing decisive results in battle, the war will be prolonged, because by retaining his trade uninjured the enemy retains all his money power to keep up his armed forces.

[107] The establishment and maintenance of the blockade therefore was, in the judgment of the present writer, not only the first step in order, but also the first, by far, in importance, open to the Government of the United States as things were; prior, that is, to the arrival of Cervera's division at some known and accessible point. Its importance lay in its twofold tendency; to exhaust the enemy's army in Cuba, and to force his navy to come to the relief. No effect more decisive than these two could be produced by us before the coming of the hostile navy, or the readiness of our own army to take the field, permitted the contest to be brought, using the words of our Italian commentator, "to an immediate issue." Upon the blockade, therefore, the generally accepted principles of warfare would demand that effort should be concentrated, until some evident radical change in the conditions dictated a change of object,—a new objective; upon which, when accepted, effort should again be concentrated, with a certain amount of "exclusiveness of purpose."

Blockade, however, implies not merely a sufficient number of cruisers to prevent the entry or departure of merchant ships. It [108] further implies, because it requires, a strong supporting force sufficient to resist being driven off by an attack from within or from without the port; for it is an accepted tenet of international law that a blockade raised by force ceases to exist, and cannot be considered re-established until a new proclamation and reoccupancy of the ground in force. Hence it follows that, prior to such re-establishment, merchant vessels trying to enter or to depart cannot be captured in virtue of the previous proclamation. Consequent upon this requirement, therefore, the blockades on the north and on the south side, to be secure against this military accident, should each have been supported by a division of armored ships capable of meeting Cervera's division on fairly equal terms; for, considering the sea distance between Cienfuegos and Havana, one such division could not support both blockades. It has already been indicated why it was impossible so to sustain the Cienfuegos blockaders. The reason, in the last analysis, was our insufficient sea-coast fortification. The Flying Squadron was kept in Hampton Roads to calm the fears of the seaboard, and to check any enterprise [109] there of Cervera, if intended or attempted. The other division of the armored fleet, however, was placed before Havana, where its presence not only strengthened adequately the blockading force proper, but assured also the safety of our naval base at Key West, both objects being attainable by the same squadron, on account of their nearness to each other.

It should likewise be noticed that the same principle of concentration of effort upon the single purpose—the blockade—forbade, *a priori*, any attempts at bombardment by which our armored ships should be brought within range of disablement by heavy guns on shore. If the blockade was our object, rightly or wrongly, and if a blockade, to be secure against serious disturbance, required all the armored ships at our disposal,—as it did,—it follows logically and rigorously that to risk those ships by attacking forts is false to principle, unless special reasons can be adduced sufficiently strong to bring such action within the scope of the principle properly applied. It is here necessary clearly to distinguish. Sound principles in warfare are as useful and as [110] necessary as in morals; when established, the presumption in any case is all on their side, and there is no one of them better established than concentration. But as in morals, so in war, the application of principle, the certainty of right, is not always clear. Could it always be, war would be an exact science; which it is not, but an art, in which true artists are as few as in painting or sculpture. It may be that a bombardment of the fortifications of Havana, or of some other place, might have been expedient, for reasons unknown to the writer; but it is clearly and decisively his opinion that if it would have entailed even a remote risk of serious injury to an armored ship, it stood condemned irretrievably (unless it conduced to getting at the enemy's navy), because it would hazard the maintenance of the blockade, our chosen object, upon which our efforts should be concentrated. [2] There is concentration of [111] purpose, as well as concentration in place, and ex-centric action in either sphere is contrary to sound military principle.

The question of keeping the armored division under Admiral Sampson in the immediate neighborhood of Havana, for the purpose of supporting the blockade by the lighter vessels, was one upon which some diversity of opinion might be expected to arise. Cervera's destination was believed—as it turned out, rightly believed—to be the West Indies. His precise point of arrival was a matter of inference only, as in fact was his general purpose. A natural surmise was that he would go first to Puerto Rico, for reasons previously indicated. But if coal enough remained to him, it was very possible that he might push on at once to his ultimate objective, if that were a Cuban port, thus avoiding the betrayal of his presence at all until within striking distance of his objective. That he could get to the United States coast without first entering a coaling [112] port, whence he would be reported, was antecedently most improbable; and, indeed, it was fair to suppose that, if bound to Havana, coal exigencies would compel him to take a pretty short route, and to pass within scouting range of the Windward Passage, between Cuba and Haïti. Whatever the particular course of reasoning, it was decided that a squadron under Admiral Sampson's command should proceed to the Windward Passage for the purpose of observation, with a view to going further eastward if it should appear advisable. Accordingly, on the 4th of May, five days after Cervera left the Cape de Verde, the Admiral sailed for the appointed position, taking with him all his armored sea-going ships—the *Iowa*, the *Indiana*, and the *New York*—and two monitors, the *Amphitrite* and the *Terror*. Of course, some smaller cruisers and a collier accompanied him.

It is almost too obvious for mention that this movement, if undertaken at all, should be made, as it was, with all the force disposable, this being too small to be safely divided. The monitors promptly, though passively, proceeded to enforce another ancient maritime [113] teaching,—the necessity for homogeneousness, especially of speed and manœuvring qualities, in vessels intending to act together. Of inferior speed at the best, they had, owing to their small coal endurance, and to minimize the delay in the progress of the whole body, consequent upon their stopping frequently to coal, to be towed each by an armored ship,—an expedient which, although the best that could be adopted, entailed endless trouble and frequent stoppages through the breaking of the tow-lines.

ToList
Shortly before midnight of May 7th, the squadron was twenty miles north of Cape Haïtien, about six hundred sea miles east of Havana. It was there learned, by telegrams received from the Department, that no information had yet been obtained as to the movements of the Spanish division, but that two swift steamers, lately of the American Transatlantic line, had been sent to scout to the eastward of Martinique and Guadaloupe. The instructions to these vessels were to cruise along a north and south line, eighty miles from the islands named. They met at the middle once a day, communicated, and then went back in opposite [114] directions to the extremities of the beat. In case the enemy were discovered, word of course would be sent from the nearest cable port to Washington, and to the Admiral, if accessible. The two vessels were directed to continue on this service up to a certain time, which was carefully calculated to meet the extreme possibilities of slowness on the part of the Spanish division, if coming that way; afterwards they were to go to a given place, and report. It may be added that they remained their full time, and yet missed by a hair's breadth sighting the enemy. The captain of one of them, the *Harvard*, afterwards told the writer that he believed another stretch to the south would have rewarded him with success. The case was one in which blame could be imputed to nobody; unless it were to the Spaniards, in disappointing our very modest expectations concerning their speed as a squadron, which is a very different thing from the speed of a single ship.

Among the telegrams received at this time by the Admiral from the Department were reports of rumors that colliers for the Spanish division had been seen near Guadaloupe; also [115] that Spanish vessels were coaling and loading ammunition at St. Thomas. Neither of these was well founded, nor was it likely that the enemy's division would pause for such purpose at a neutral island, distant, as St. Thomas is, less than one hundred miles from their own harbors in Puerto Rico.

Immediately after the receipt of these telegrams, the Admiral summoned all his captains between 12 and 4 A.M., May 9th, to a consultation regarding the situation. He then decided to go on to San Juan, the chief seaport of Puerto Rico, upon the chance of finding the Spanish squadron there. The coaling of the monitors, which had begun when the squadron stopped the previous afternoon, was resumed next morning. At 11.15, May 9th, a telegram from the Department reported a story, "published in the newspapers," that the Spanish division had been seen on the night of the 7th, near Martinique. The Department's telegram betrayed also some anxiety about Key West and the Havana blockade; but, while urging a speedy return, the details of the Admiral's movements were left to his own discretion. The squadron then stood east, and on the [116] early morning of the 12th arrived off San Juan. An attack upon the forts followed at once, lasting from 5.30 to 7.45 A.M.; but, as it was evident that the

Spanish division was not there, the Admiral decided not to continue the attack, although satisfied that he could force a surrender. His reasons for desisting are given in his official report as follows:— "The fact that we should be held several days in completing arrangements for holding the place; that part [of the squadron] would have to be left to await the arrival of troops to garrison it; that the movements of the Spanish squadron, our main objective, were still unknown; that the Flying Squadron was still north and not in a position to render any aid; that Havana, Cervera's natural objective, was thus open to entry by such a force as his, while we were a thousand miles distant,—made our immediate movement toward Havana imperative."

It will be noted that the Admiral's conclusions, as here given, coincided substantially with the feeling of the Department as expressed in the telegram last mentioned. The squadron started back immediately to the westward. During the night of this same day, Thursday, May 12th, towards midnight, [117] reliable information was received at the Navy Department that Cervera's squadron had arrived off Martinique,—four armored cruisers and three torpedo destroyers, one of the latter entering the principal port of the island.

The movements of the Spanish division immediately preceding its appearance off Martinique can be recovered in the main from the log of the *Cristobal Colon*, which was found on board that ship by the United States officers upon taking possession after her surrender on July 3. Some uncertainty attends the conclusions reached from its examination, because the record is brief and not always precise in its statements; but, whatever inaccuracy of detail there may be, the general result is clear enough.

At noon on May 10th the division was one hundred and thirty miles east of the longitude of Martinique, and fifteen miles south of its southernmost point. Being thus within twelve hours' run of the island, Admiral Cervera evidently, and reasonably, considered that he might now be in the neighborhood of danger, if the United States Government had decided to attempt to intercept him with an armored division, instead of sticking to the dispositions [118] known to him when he sailed,—the blockade of Cuba and the holding the Flying Squadron in reserve. In order not to fall in with an enemy unexpectedly, especially during the night, the speed of the division was reduced to something less than four knots, and the torpedo destroyer *Terror* was sent ahead to reconnoitre and report. The incident of her separating from her consorts is not noted,—a singular omission, due possibly to its occurring at night and so escaping observation by the *Colon*; but it is duly logged that she was sighted "to port" next morning, May 11th, at 9 A. M., and that, until she was recognized, the crew were sent to their quarters for action. This precaution had also been observed during the previous night, the men sleeping beside their guns,—a sufficient evidence of the suspicions entertained by the Spanish Admiral.

At 10 A.M.—by which hour, or very soon afterwards, the communication of the *Terror* with the Admiral recorded by the log must have taken place—there had been abundance of time since daybreak for a 15-knot torpedo destroyer, low-lying in the water, to remain unseen within easy scouting distance of [119] Martinique, and thence to rejoin the squadron, which would then be forty or fifty miles distant from the island. She could even, by putting forth all her speed, have communicated with the shore; possibly without the knowledge of the American representatives on the spot, if the sympathies of the inhabitants were with the Spaniards, as has been generally believed. However that may be, shortly after her junction the division went ahead again seven knots, the speed logged at noon of May 11th, which, as steam formed, was increased to ten knots. At 4 P.M. Martinique was abeam on the starboard hand—north. At sundown the ships went to general quarters, and the crews were again kept at their guns during the night. By this time Cervera doubtless had been informed that Sampson's division had gone east from Cuba, but its destination could have been only a matter of inference with him, for the attack upon San Juan did not take place till the following morning. The fact of keeping his men at quarters also justifies the conclusion that he was thus uncertain about Sampson, for the stationariness of the Flying Squadron would be known at Martinique.

[120] After mentioning that the ship's company went to quarters, the log of the *Colon* adds: "Stopped from 5.15 to 6 A.M." Whether the 5.15 was A.M. or P.M., whether, in short, the squadron continued practically motionless during the night of May 11th-12th, can only be conjectured, but there can be little doubt that it did so remain. The Spaniards still observe the old-fashioned sea-day of a century ago, abandoned long since by the British and ourselves, according to which May 12th begins at noon of May 11th. A continuous transaction, such as stopping from evening to morning, would fall, therefore, in the log of the same day, as it here does; whereas in a United States ship of war, even were our records as brief and fragmentary as the *Colon*'s, the fact of the stoppage, extending over the logs of two days, would have been mentioned in each. It is odd, after passing an hour or two in putting this and that together out of so incomplete a narrative, to find recorded in full, a few days later, the following notable incident: "At 2.30 P.M. flagship made signal: 'If you want fresh beef, send boat.' Answered: 'Many thanks; do not require any.'" Log-books do state [121] such occurrences, particularly when matters of signal; but then they are supposed also to give a reasonably full account of each day's important proceedings.

Whatever the movements back and forth, or the absence of movement, by the Spanish ships during the night, at 7.10 A.M. the next day, May 12th, while Sampson's division was still engaged with the forts at San Juan, they were close to Martinique, "four miles from Diamond Rock," a detached islet at its southern end. The next entry, the first for the sea-day of May 13th, is: "At 12. 20 P.M. lost sight of Martinique." As the land there is high enough to be visible forty or fifty miles under favorable conditions, and as the squadron on its way to Curaçao averaged 11 knots per hour, it seems reasonable to infer that the Spanish Admiral, having received news of the attack on San Juan, though possibly not of the result, had determined upon a hasty departure and a hurried run to the end of his journey, before he could be intercepted by Sampson, the original speed of whose ships was inferior to that of his own, and whom he knew to be hampered by monitors.

The Spaniards did not take coal at [122] Martinique. This may have been due to refusal by the French officials to permit it, according to a common neutral rule which allows a neutral only to give enough to reach the nearest national port. As the ships still had enough to reach Curaçao, they had more than enough to go to Puerto Rico. It may very well be, also, that Cervera, not caring to meet Sampson, whose force, counting the monitors, was superior to his own, thought best to disappear at once again from our knowledge. He did indeed prolong his journey to Santiago, if that were his original destination, by nearly two hundred miles, through going to Curaçao; not to speak of the delay there in coaling. But, if the Dutch allowed him to take all that he wanted, he would in his final start be much nearer Cuba than at Martinique, and he would be able, as far as fuel went, to reach either Santiago, Cienfuegos, or Puerto Rico, or even Havana itself,—all which possibilities would tend to perplex us. It is scarcely probable, however, that he would have attempted the last-named port. To do so, not to speak of the greater hazard through the greater distance, would, in case of his success, not merely have enabled, but [123] invited, the United States to concentrate its fleet in the very best position for us, where it would not only have "contained" the enemy, but have best protected our own base at Key West.

In the absence of certain knowledge, conjectural opinions, such as the writer has here educed, are not unprofitable; rather the reverse. To form them, the writer and the reader place themselves perforce nearly in Cervera's actual position, and pass through their own minds the grist of unsolved difficulties which confronted him. The result of such a process is a much more real mental possession than is yielded by a quiet perusal of any ascertained facts, because it involves an argumentative consideration of opposing conditions, and not a mere passive acceptance of statements. The general conclusion of the present writer, from this consideration of Cervera's position, and of that of our own Government, is that the course of the Spanish Admiral was opportunist, solely and simply. Such, in general, and necessarily, must be that of any "fleet in being," in the strict sense of the phrase, which involves inferiority of force; whereas the stronger force, if handled with sagacity and strength, constrains the [124] weaker in its orbit as the earth governs the moon. Placed in an extremely false position by the fault, militarily unpardonable, of his Government, Admiral Cervera doubtless did the best he could. That in so doing he caused the United States authorities to pass through some moments of perplexity is certain, but it was the perplexity of interest rather than of apprehension; and in so far as the latter was felt at all, it was due to antecedent faults of disposition on our own part, the causes of which have been in great measure indicated already. The writer is not an angler, but he understands that there is an anxious pleasure in the suspense of playing a fish, as in any important contest involving skill.

To say that there was any remarkable merit in the movements of the Spanish Admiral is as absurd as to attribute particular cleverness to a child who, with his hands behind his back, asks the old conundrum, "Right or left?" "It is all a matter of guess," said Nelson, "and the world attributes wisdom to him who guesses right;" but all the same, by unremitting watchfulness, sagacious inference, and diligent pursuit, he ran the French fleet [125] down. At Martinique, Admiral Cervera had all the West Indies before him where to choose, and the United States coast too, conditioned by coal and other needs, foreseen or unforeseen. We ran him down at Santiago; and had he vanished from there, we should have caught him somewhere else. The attempt of the Spanish authorities to create an impression that some marvellous feat of strategy was in process of execution, to the extreme discomfiture of the United States navy, was natural enough, considering the straits they were in, and the consciousness of the capable among them that a squadron of that force never should have been sent across the sea; but, though natural, the pretension was absurd, and, though echoed by all the partisan Press in Europe, it did not for a moment impose as true upon those who were directing the movements of the United States ships.

FOOTNOTES:

[2] A principal object of these papers, as has been stated, is to form a correct public opinion; for by public opinion, if misguided, great embarrassment is often caused to those responsible for the conduct of a war. As concrete examples teach far better than abstract principles, the writer suggests to the consideration of his readers how seriously would have been felt, during the hostilities, the accident which befell the battleship *Massachusetts*, on Dec. 14, 1898, a month after the above sentences were written. An injury in battle, engaged without adequate object, would have had the same effect, and been indefensible.

[126]

IV ToC

Problems Presented by Cervera's Appearance in West Indian Waters.—Movements of the United States Divisions and of the Oregon.—Functions of Cruisers in a Naval Campaign.

The departure of Admiral Cervera from Martinique for Curaçao was almost simultaneous with that of Admiral Sampson from San Juan for Key West. The immediate return of the latter to the westward was dictated by reasons, already given in his own words, the weight of which he doubtless felt more forcibly because he found himself actually so far away from the centre of the blockade and from his base at Key West. When he began thus to retrace his steps, he was still ignorant of Cervera's arrival. The following night, indeed, he heard from a passing vessel the rumor of the Spanish squadron's regaining Cadiz, with which the Navy Department had been for a moment amused. He stopped, therefore, to communicate with Washington, intending, if the rumor were confirmed, to resume the attack upon San Juan. But on the [127] morning of the 15th—Sunday—at 3.30, his despatch-boat returned to him with the official intelligence, not only of the enemy's being off Martinique, but of his arrival at Curaçao, which occurred shortly after daylight of the 14th. The same telegram informed him that the Flying Squadron was on its way to Key West, and directed him to regain that point himself with all possible rapidity.

Cervera left behind him at Martinique one of his torpedo destroyers, the *Terror*. A demonstration was made by this vessel, probably, though it may have been by one of her fellows, before St. Pierre,—another port of the island,—where the *Harvard* was lying; and as the latter had been sent hurriedly from home with but a trifling battery, some anxiety was felt lest the enemy might score a point upon her, if the local authorities compelled her to leave. If the Spaniard had been as fast as represented, he would have had an advantage over the American in both speed and armament,—very serious odds. The machinery of the former, however, was in bad order, and she soon had to seek a harbor in Fort de France, also in Martinique; after which [128] the usual rule, that two belligerents may not leave the same neutral port within twenty-four hours of each other, assured the *Harvard* a safe start. This incident, otherwise trivial, is worthy of note, for it shows one of the results of our imperfect national preparation for war. If the conditions had allowed time to equip the *Harvard* with suitable guns, she could have repulsed such an enemy, as a ship of the same class, the *St. Paul*, did a few weeks later off San Juan, whither the *Terror* afterwards repaired, and where she remained till the war was over.

The news of Cervera's appearance off Martinique was first received at the Navy Department about midnight of May 12th-13th, nearly thirty-six hours after the fact. As our representatives there, and generally throughout the West Indies, were very much on the alert, it seems not improbable that their telegrams, to say the least, were not given undue precedence of other matters. That, however, is one of the chances of life, and most especially of war. It is more to the purpose, because more useful to future guidance, to consider the general situation at the moment the telegram was received, [129] the means at hand to meet the exigencies of the case, and what instructive light is thereby thrown back upon preceding movements, which had resulted in the actual conditions.

Admiral Cervera's division had been at Martinique, and, after a brief period of suspense, was known to have disappeared to the westward. The direction taken, however, might, nay, almost certainly must, be misleading,—that was part of his game. From it nothing could be decisively inferred. The last news of the *Oregon* was that she had left Bahia, in Brazil, on the 9th of the month. Her whereabouts and intended movements were as unknown to the United States authorities as to the enemy. An obvious precaution, to assure getting assistance to her, would have been to prescribe the exact route she should follow, subject only to the conditional discretion which can never wisely be taken from the officer in command on the spot. In that way it would have been possible to send a division to meet her, if indications at any moment countenanced the suspicion entertained by some—the author among others—that Cervera would attempt to intercept her. After careful consideration, this [130] precaution had not been attempted, because the tight censorship of the Press had not then been effectually enforced, and it was feared that even so vital and evident a necessity as that of concealing her movements would not avail against the desire of some newspapers to manifest enterprise, at whatever cost to national interests. If we ever again get into a serious war, a close supervision of the Press, punitive as well as preventive, will be one of the first military necessities, unless the tone and disposition, not of the best, but of the worst, of its members shall have become sensibly improved; for occasional unintentional leakage, by well-meaning officials possessing more information than native secretiveness, cannot be wholly obviated, and must be accepted, practically, as one of the inevitable difficulties of conducting war.

The *Oregon*, therefore, was left a loose end, and was considered to be safer so than if more closely looked after. From the time she left Bahia till she arrived at Barbados, and from thence till she turned up off Jupiter Inlet, on the Florida coast, no one in Washington knew where she was. Nevertheless, she continued [131] a most important and exposed fraction of the national naval force. That Cervera had turned west when last seen from Martinique meant nothing. It was more significant and reassuring to know that he had not got coal there. Still, it was possible that he might take a chance off Barbados, trusting, as he with perfect reason could, that when he had waited there as long as his coal then on hand permitted, the British authorities would let him take enough more to reach Puerto Rico, as they did give Captain Clark sufficient to gain a United States port. When the *Oregon* got to Barbados at 3.20 A.M. of May 18th, less than six days had elapsed since Cervera quitted Martinique; and the two islands are barely one hundred miles apart. All this, of course, is very much more clear to our present knowledge than it could possibly be to the Spanish Admiral, who probably, and not unnaturally, thought it far better to get his "fleet in being" under the guns of a friendly port than to hazard it on what might prove a wild-goose chase; for, after all, Captain Clark might not have gone to Barbados.

It may be interesting to the reader to say [132] here that the Navy Department,—which was as much in the dark as Cervera himself,—although it was necessarily concerned about the *Oregon*, and gave much thought to the problem how best to assure her safety, was comforted by the certainty that, whatever befell the ship, the national interests would not be gravely compromised if she did meet the enemy. The situation was not novel or unprecedented, and historical precedents are an immense support to the spirit in doubtful moments. Conscious of the power of the ship herself, and confident in her captain and officers, whom it knew well, the Department was assured, to use words of Nelson when he was expecting to be similarly outnumbered, "Before we are destroyed, I have little doubt but the enemy will have their wings so completely clipped that they will be easily overtaken." Such odds for our ship were certainly not desired; but, the best having been done that could be in the circumstances, there was reasonable ground to believe that, by the time the enemy got through with her, they would not amount to much as a fighting squadron.

Some little while after the return of [133] Admiral Sampson's squadron to New York, the writer chanced to see, quoted as an after-dinner speech by the chief engineer of the *Oregon*, the statement that Captain Clark had communicated to his officers the tactics he meant to pursue, if he fell in with the Spanish division. His purpose, as so explained, deserves to be noted; for it assures our people, if they need any further assurance, that in the single ship, as in the squadrons, intelligent skill as well as courage presided in the councils of the officers in charge. The probability was that the Spanish vessels, though all reputed faster than the *Oregon*, had different rates of speed, and each singly was inferior to her in fighting force, in addition to which the American ship had a very heavy stern battery. The intention therefore was, in case of a meeting, to turn the stern to the enemy and to make a running fight. This not only gave a superiority of fire to the *Oregon* so long as the relative positions lasted, but it tended, of course, to prolong it, confining the enemy to their bow fire and postponing to the utmost possible the time of their drawing near enough to open with the broadside rapid-fire batteries. [134] Moreover, if the Spanish vessels were not equally fast, and if their rate of speed did not much exceed that of the *Oregon*, both very probable conditions, it was quite possible that in the course of the action the leading ship would outstrip her followers so much as to be engaged singly, and even that two or more might thus be successively beaten in detail. If it be replied that this is assuming a great deal, and attributing stupidity to the enemy, the answer is that the result here supposed has not infrequently followed upon similar action, and that war is full of uncertainties,—an instance again of the benefit and comfort which some historical acquaintance with the experience of others imparts to a man engaged with present perplexities. Deliberately to incur such odds would be unjustifiable; but when unavoidably confronted with them, resolution enlightened by knowledge may dare still to hope.

An instructive instance of drawing such support from the very fountain heads of military history, in the remote and even legendary past, is given by Captain Clark in a letter replying to inquiries from the present writer:—

"There is little to add to what you already know about the [135] way I hoped to fight Cervera's fleet, if we fell in with it. What I feared was that he would be able to bring his ships up within range together, supposing that the slowest was faster than the *Oregon*; but there was the chance that their machinery was in different stages of deterioration, and there was also the hope that impetuosity or excitement might after a time make some press on in advance of the others. I, of course, had in mind the tactics of the last of the Horatii, and hopefully referred to them. The announcement Milligan (the chief engineer) spoke of was made before we reached Bahia, I think before we turned Cape Frio, as it was off that headland that I decided to leave the *Marietta* and *Nictheroy*, (now the *Buffalo*), and to push on alone. You may be sure that was an anxious night for me when I decided to part company. The Department was, of course, obliged to leave much to my discretion, and I knew that the Spaniards might all close to rapid-fire range, overpower all but our turret guns, and then send in their torpedo boats."

It was upon the *Marietta* that he had previously depended, in a measure, to thwart the attacks of these small vessels; but in such a contest as that with four armored cruisers she could scarcely count, and she was delaying his progress in the run immediately before him.

"The torpedo boat [he continues] was a rattlesnake to me, [136] that I feared would get in his work while I was fighting the tiger; but I felt that the chances were that Cervera was bound to the West Indies, and so that the need of the *Oregon* there was so great that the risk of his turning south to meet me should be run, so I hurried to Bahia, and cabled to the Department my opinion of what the *Oregon* might do alone and in a running fight. My object was to add the *Oregon* to our fleet, and not to meet the Spaniards, if it could be avoided."

It may be added that in this his intention coincided with the wish of the Department.

"So when, in Barbados, the reports came off that the Spanish fleet (and rumors had greatly increased its size) was at Martinique, that three torpedo boats had been seen from the island, I ordered coal to be loaded till after midnight, but left soon after dark, started west, then turned and went around the island"—that is, well to the eastward—"and made to the northward."

This was on the evening of May 18th. Six days later the ship was off the coast of Florida, and in communication with the Department.

The *Oregon* may properly be regarded as one of the three principal detachments into [137] which the United States fleet was divided at the opening of the eventful week, May 12th-19th, and which, however they might afterwards be distributed around the strategic centre,—which we had chosen should be about Havana and Cienfuegos,—needed to be brought to it as rapidly as possible. No time was avoidably lost. On the evening of May 13th, eighteen hours after Cervera's appearance at Martinique was reported, the two larger divisions, under Sampson and Schley, were consciously converging upon our point of concentration at Key West; while the third, the *Oregon*, far more distant, was also moving to the same place in the purpose of the Department, though, as yet, unconsciously to herself. Sampson had over twenty-four hours' start of the Flying Squadron; and the distances to be traversed, from Puerto Rico and Hampton Roads, were practically the same. [3] But the former was much delayed by the slowness of the monitors, and, great as he felt the need of haste to be, and urgent as was the Department's telegram, received on the 15th, [138] he very properly would not allow his vessels to separate until nearer their destination. Precautionary orders were sent by him to the *Harvard* and *Yale*—two swift despatch vessels then under his immediate orders—to coal to the utmost and to hold themselves at the end of a cable ready for immediate orders; while Commodore Remey, commanding at Key West, was directed to have every preparation complete for coaling the squadron on the 18th, when it might be expected to arrive. The *St. Louis*, a vessel of the same type as the *Harvard*, met the Admiral while these telegrams were being written. She was ordered to cut the cables at Santiago and Guantanamo Bay, and afterwards at Ponce, Puerto Rico.

The Flying Squadron had sailed at 4 P.M. of the 13th. Its fighting force consisted of the *Brooklyn*, armored cruiser, flagship; the *Massachusetts*, first-class, and the *Texas*, second-class, battleships. It is to be inferred from the departure of these vessels that the alarm about our own coast, felt while the whereabouts of the hostile division was unknown, vanished when it made its appearance. The result was, perhaps, not strictly logical; [139] but the logic of the step is of less consequence than its undoubted military correctness. We had chosen our objective, and now we were concentrating upon it,—a measure delayed too long, though unavoidably. Commodore Schley was directed to call off Charleston for orders; for, while it is essential to have a settled strategic idea in any campaign, it is also necessary, in maritime warfare, at all events, to be ready to change a purpose suddenly and to turn at once upon the great objective,—which dominates and supersedes all others,—the enemy's navy, when a reasonable prospect of destroying it, or any large fraction of it, offers. When Schley left Hampton Roads, it was known only that the Spanish division had appeared off Martinique. The general intention, that our own should go to Key West, must therefore be held subject to possible modification, and to that end communication at a half-way point was imperative. No detention was thereby caused. At 4.30 P.M. of the 15th the Flying Squadron, which had been somewhat delayed by ten hours of dense fog, came off Charleston Bar, where a lighthouse steamer had been waiting since the previous midnight. From the officer in charge [140] of her the Commodore received his orders, and at 6 P.M. was again under way for Key West, where he arrived on the 18th, anticipating by several hours Sampson's arrival in person, and by a day the coming of the slower ships of the other division.

But if it is desirable to ensure frequent direct communication with the larger divisions of the fleet, at such a moment, when their movements must be held subject to sudden change to meet the as yet uncertain developments of the enemy's strategy, it is still more essential to keep touch from a central station with the swift single cruisers, the purveyors of intelligence and distributors of the information upon which the conduct of the war depends. If the broad strategic conception of the naval campaign is correct, and the consequent action consistent, the greater fighting units—squadrons or fleets—may be well, or better, left to themselves, after the initial impulse of direction is given, and general instructions have been issued to their commanders. These greater units, however, cannot usually be kept at the end of a telegraph cable; yet they must, through cables, maintain, with their centres of [141] intelligence, communication so frequent as to be practically constant. The Flying Squadron when off Cienfuegos, and Admiral Sampson's division at the time now under consideration, while on its passage from San Juan to Key West, are instances in point. Conversely, dependence may be placed upon local agents to report an enemy when he enters port; but when at sea for an unknown destination, it is necessary, if practicable, to get and keep touch with him, and to have his movements, actual and probable, reported. In short, steady communication must be maintained, as far as possible, between the always fixed points where the cables end, and the more variable positions where the enemy's squadrons and our own are, whether for a stay or in transit. This can be done only through swift despatch vessels; and for these, great as is the need that no time be wasted in their missions, the homely proverb, "more haste, less speed," has to be kept in mind. To stop off at a wayside port, to diverge even considerably from the shortest route, may often be a real economy of time.

The office of cruisers thus employed is to substitute certainty for conjecture; to correct [142] or to confirm, by fuller knowledge, the inferences upon which the conduct of operations otherwise so much depends. Accurate intelligence is one of the very first *desiderata* of war, and as the means of obtaining and transmitting it are never in excess of the necessities, those means have to be carefully administered. Historically, no navy ever has had cruisers enough; partly because the lookout and despatch duties themselves are so extensive and onerous; partly because vessels of the class are wanted for other purposes also,—as, for instance, in our late war, for the blockade of the Cuban ports, which was never much more than technically "effective," and for the patrolling of our Atlantic seaboard. True economical use of the disposable vessels, obtaining the largest results with the least expenditure of means never adequate, demands much forethought and more management, and is best effected by so arranging that the individual cruisers can be quickly got hold of when wanted. This is accomplished by requiring them to call at cable ports and report; or by circumscribing the area in which they are to cruise, so that they can be readily found; or by prescribing the [143] course and speed they are to observe,— in short, by ensuring a pretty close knowledge of their position at every moment.

For the purposes of intelligence, a cruiser with a roving commission, or one which neglects to report its movements when opportunity offers, is nearly useless; and few things are more justly exasperating than the failure of a cruiser to realize this truth in practice. Of course, no rule is hard and fast to bind the high discretion of the officer senior on the spot; but if the captains of cruisers will bear in mind, as a primary principle, that they, their admirals, and the central office, are in this respect parts of one highly specialized and most important system in which co-operation must be observed, discretion will more rarely err in these matters, where errors may be so serious. That with a central office, admirals, and captains, all seeking the same ends, matters will at times work at cross purposes, only proves the common experience that things will not always go straight here below. When Nelson was hunting for the French fleet before the battle of the Nile, his flagship was dismasted in a gale of wind off Corsica. The commander of the [144] frigates, his lookout ships, having become separated in the gale, concluded that the Admiral would have to return to Gibraltar, and took his frigates there. "I thought he knew me better," commented Nelson. "Every moment I have to regret the frigates having left me," he wrote later; "the return to Syracuse," due to want of intelligence, "broke my heart, which on any extraordinary anxiety now shows itself." It is not possible strictly to define official discretion, nor to guard infallibly against its misuse; but, all the same, it is injurious to an officer to show that he lacks sound judgment.

When the Flying Squadron sailed, there were lying in Hampton Roads three swift cruisers,—the *New Orleans*, the *St. Paul*, and the *Minneapolis*. Two auxiliary cruisers, the *Yosemite* and the *Dixie*, were nearly but not quite ready for sea. It was for some time justly considered imperative to keep one such ship there ready for an immediate mission. The *New Orleans* was so retained, subject to further requirements of the Department; but the *Minneapolis* and the *St. Paul* sailed as soon as their coaling was completed,—within [145] twenty-four hours of the squadron. The former was to cruise between Haïti and the Caicos Bank, on the road which Cervera would probably follow if he went north of Haïti; the other was to watch between Haïti and Jamaica, where he might be encountered if he took the Windward Passage, going south of Haïti. At the time these orders were issued the indications were that the Spanish division was hanging about Martinique, hoping for permission to coal there; and as both of our cruisers were very fast vessels and directed to go at full speed, the chances were more than good that they would reach their cruising ground before Cervera could pass it.

These intended movements were telegraphed to Sampson, and it was added, "Very important that your fast cruisers keep touch with the Spanish squadron." This he received May 15th. With his still imperfect information he gave no immediate orders which would lose him his hold of the *Harvard* and the *Yale*; but shortly after midnight he learned, off Cape Haïtien, that the Spanish division was to have left Curaçao the previous evening at six o'clock—only six hours before this despatch reached [146] him. He at once cabled the *Harvard* and the *Yale*, to which, as being under his immediate charge, the Department had given no orders, to go to sea, the former to cruise in the Mona Passage, to detect the enemy if he passed through it for Puerto Rico, the *Yale* to assist the *St. Paul* at the station of which he had been notified from Washington. The Department was informed by him of these dispositions. Sampson at the same time cabled Remey at Key West to warn the blockaders off Cienfuegos— none of which were armored—of the possible appearance of the enemy at that port. In this step he had been anticipated by the Department, which, feeling the urgency of the case and uncertain of communicating betimes through him, had issued an order direct to Remey, thirty-six hours before, that those ships, with a single exception, should be withdrawn; and that the vessels on the north coast should be notified, but not removed.

These various movements indicate the usefulness and the employments of the cruiser class, one of which also carried the news to Cienfuegos, another along the north coast, while a third took Sampson's telegrams from [147] his position at sea to the cable port. Owing to our insufficient number of vessels of the kind required, torpedo boats, of great speed in smooth water, but of delicate machinery and liable to serious retardation in a sea-way, were much used for these missions, to the great hurt of their engines, not intended for long-continued high exertion, and to their own consequent injury for their particular duties. The *St. Paul's* career exemplified also the changes of direction to which cruisers are liable, and the consequent necessity of keeping them well in hand both as regards position and preparation, especially of coal. Between the time the *Minneapolis* sailed and her own departure, at 6 P.M., of May 14th, the news of the Spanish division's arrival at Curaçao was received; and as there had been previous independent information that colliers had been ordered to meet it in the Gulf of Venezuela, only a hundred miles from Curaçao, the conclusion was fair that the enemy needed coal and hoped to get it in that neighborhood. Why else, indeed, if as fast as reported, and aware, as he must be, that Sampson was as far east as San Juan, had he not pushed direct for Cuba, his probable [148] objective? In regard to colliers being due in the Gulf of Venezuela, the reports proved incorrect; but the inference as to the need of coal was accurate, and that meant delay. The *St. Paul* was therefore ordered to Key West, instructions being telegraphed there to coal her full immediately on arriving. She would there be as near the Windward Passage as Curaçao is, and yet able, in case of necessity, to proceed by the Yucatan Passage or in any direction that might meanwhile become expedient. It may be added that the *St. Paul* reached Key West and was coaled ready for sea by the evening of May 18th, four days from the time she left Hampton Roads, a thousand miles distant.

While on her passage, the Department had entertained the purpose of sending her to the Gulf of Venezuela and adding to her the *Harvard* and the *Minneapolis*, the object being not only to find the enemy, if there, but that one of the three should report him, while the other two dogged his path until no doubt of his destination could remain. Their great speed, considered relatively to that which the enemy had so far shown, gave reasonable probability [149] that thus his approach could be communicated by them, and by cables, throughout the whole field of operations, with such rapidity as to ensure cornering him at once, which was the first great essential of our campaign. A cruiser reporting at Cape Haïtien was picked up and sent to the *Minneapolis*, whose whereabouts was sufficiently known, because circumscribed, and she received her orders; but they served only to develop the weakness of that ship and of the *Columbia*, considered as cruisers. The coal left after her rapid steaming to her cruising ground did not justify the further sweep required, and her captain thought it imperative to go first to St. Thomas to recoal,—a process which involved more delay than on the surface appears. The bunkers of this ship and of her sister, the *Columbia*, are minutely subdivided,—an arrangement very suitable, even imperative, in a battleship, in order to localize strictly any injury received in battle, but inconsequent and illogical in a vessel meant primarily for speed. A moment's reflection upon the services required of cruisers will show that their efficiency does not depend merely upon rapid going through the water, but upon prompt readiness [150] to leave port, of which promptness quick coaling is a most important factor. This is gravely retarded by bunkers much subdivided. The design of these two ships, meant for speed, involves this lack of facility for recoaling. There is, therefore, in them a grave failure in that unity of conception which should dominate all designs.

The movements, actual and projected, of the cruisers at this moment have purposely been dwelt upon at some length. Such movements and the management of them play a most important part in all campaigns, and it is desirable that they should be understood, through illustration such as this; because the provision for the service should be antecedently thorough and consistent in plan and in execution, in order to efficiency. Confusion of thought, and consequent confusion of object, is fatal to any conception,—at least, to any military conception; it is absolutely opposed to concentration, for it implies duality of object. In the designing of a cruiser, as of any class of warship, the first step, before which none should be taken, is to decide the primary object to be realized,—what is this ship [151] meant to do? To this primary requirement every other feature should be subordinated. Its primacy is not only one of time, but of importance also. The recognition, in practice, of this requisite does not abolish nor exclude the others by its predominance. It simply regulates their development; for they not only must not militate against it, they must minister to it. It is exactly as in a novel or in a work of art, for every military conception, from the design of a ship up, should be a work of art. Perfection does not exclude a multiplicity of detail, but it does demand unity of motive, a single central idea, to which all detail is strictly accessory, to emphasize or to enhance,—not to distract. The cruiser requirements offer a concrete illustration of the application of this thought. Rapidity of action is the primary object. In it is involved both coal endurance and facility for recoaling; for each economizes time, as speed does. Defensive strength—of which subdivision of coal bunkers is an element—conduces only secondarily to rapidity of movement, as does offensive power; they must, therefore, be very strictly subordinated. They must not detract from [152] speed; yet so far as they do not injure that, they should be developed, for by the power to repel an enemy—to avert detention—they minister to rapidity. With the battleship, in this contrary to the cruiser, offensive power is the dominant feature. While, therefore, speed is desirable to it, excessive speed is not admissible, if, as the author believes, it can be obtained only at some sacrifice of offensive strength.

When Admiral Sampson sent off the telegrams last mentioned, before daylight of May 16th, the flagship was off Cape Haïtien. During her stoppage for this purpose, the squadron continued to stand west, in order not to increase the loss of time due to the slowness of the monitors, through which the progress of the whole body did not exceed from seven to eight sea miles per hour. Cape Haïtien is distant from Key West nearly seven hundred miles; and throughout this distance, being almost wholly along the coast of Cuba, no close telegraphic communication could be expected. At the squadron's rate of advance it could not count upon arriving at Key West, and so regaining touch with Washington, [153] before the morning of the 19th, and the Department was thus notified. Thirty-six hours later, at 11.30 A. M., May 17th, being then in the Old Bahama Channel, between Cuba and the Bahama Banks, the Admiral felt that his personal presence, under existing conditions, was more necessary near Havana and Key West. Leaving the division, therefore, in charge of the senior officer, Captain Evans, of the *Iowa*, he pushed forward with the flagship *New York*, the fastest of the armored vessels. Six hours later he was met by the torpedo boat *Dupont*, bringing him a telegram from the Department, dated the 16th, forwarded through Key West, directing him to send his most suitable armored ship ahead to join the Flying Squadron. This order was based on information that Cervera was bringing munitions of war essential to the defence of Havana, and that his instructions were peremptory to reach either Havana or a port connected with it by railroad. Such commands pointed evidently to Cienfuegos, which place, moreover, was clearly indicated from the beginning of the campaign, as already shown in these papers, as the station for one division of our armored fleet.

[154] The Department could calculate certainly that, by the time its message reached Sampson, his division would be so far advanced as to ensure interposing between Havana and the Spaniards, if the latter came by the Windward Passage—from the eastward. It was safe, therefore, or at least involved less risk of missing the enemy, to send the Flying Squadron to Cienfuegos, either heading him off there, or with a chance of meeting him in the Yucatan Channel, if he tried to reach Havana by going west of Cuba. But as Cienfuegos was thought the more likely destination, and was for every reason a port to be effectually blockaded, it was desirable to reinforce Schley, not by detaining him, under the pressing need of his getting to Cienfuegos, but by a battleship following him as soon as possible. Of course, such a ship might be somewhat exposed to encountering the enemy's division single-handed, which is contrary to rule. But rules are made to be broken on occasion, as well as to be observed generally; and again, and always, war cannot be made without running risks, of which the greatest is misplaced or exaggerated caution. From the moment the Spanish ships were [155] reported at Curaçao, a close lookout had been established in the Yucatan Channel.

By his personal action, in quitting his squadron in order to hasten forward, Admiral Sampson had anticipated the wishes of the Department. At 4 P.M., May 18th, he reached Key West, where he found the Flying Squadron and the *St. Paul*, anchored in the outer roads. His own telegrams, and those from the Secretary of the Navy, had ensured preparations for coaling all vessels as they arrived, to the utmost rapidity that the facilities of the port admitted. The *St. Paul*, whose orders had been again changed, sailed the same evening for Cape Haïtien. The Flying Squadron started for Cienfuegos at 9 A.M. the following day, the 19th, and was followed twenty-six hours later by the battleship *Iowa*. Shortly after the Admiral left the fleet, it had been overtaken by the torpedo boat *Porter*, from Cape Haïtien, bearing a despatch which showed the urgency of the general situation, although it in no way fettered the discretion of the officer in charge. Captain Evans, therefore, very judiciously imitated Sampson's action, quitted the fleet, and hastened with his own [156] ship to Key West, arriving at dark of the 18th. Being a vessel of large coal endurance, she did not delay there to fill up, but she took with her the collier *Merrimac* for the ships before Cienfuegos.

The remainder of Sampson's division arrived on the 19th. The monitors *Puritan* and *Miantonomoh*, which had not been to San Juan, sailed on the 20th for the Havana blockade, where they were joined before noon of the 21st by the *Indiana*, and the *New York*, the latter having the Admiral on board. Commodore Schley, with the Flying Squadron, arrived off Cienfuegos toward midnight of the same day. The *Iowa*, came up twelve hours later, about noon of the 22nd, and some four or five light cruisers joined on that or the following days. On the 24th the *Oregon* communicated with Washington off Jupiter Inlet, on the east coast of Florida. Her engines being reported perfectly ready, after her long cruise, she was directed to go to Key West, where she coaled, and on the 28th left for the Havana blockade.

It is difficult to exaggerate the honor which this result does to Chief Engineer Milligan and to the officers responsible under him for the [157] condition of her machinery. The combination of skill and care thus evidenced is of the highest order.

Such, in general outline, omitting details superfluous to correct comprehension, was the course of incidents on our side, in the Cuban campaign, during the ten days, May 12th-21st; from the bombardment of San Juan de Puerto Rico to the establishment of the two armored divisions in the positions which, under better conditions of national preparation, they should have occupied by the 1st of the month. All is well that ends well—so far at least as the wholly past is concerned; but for the instruction of the future it is necessary not to cast the past entirely behind our backs before its teachings have been pondered and assimilated. We cannot expect ever again to have an enemy so entirely inapt as Spain showed herself to be; yet, even so, Cervera's division reached Santiago on the 19th of May, two days before our divisions appeared in the full force they could muster before Havana and Cienfuegos. Had the Spanish Admiral been trying for one of those ports, even at the low rate of speed observed in going from Curaçao to [158] Santiago—about seven and five-tenth knots—he could have left Curaçao on the evening of May 15th, and have reached Cienfuegos on the 21st, between midnight and daybreak, enabling him to enter the harbor by 8 A.M. —more than twelve hours before the arrival there of our Flying Squadron.

The writer assumes that, had our coast defences been such as to put our minds at ease concerning the safety of our chief seaboard cities, the Flying Squadron would from the first have been off Cienfuegos. He is forced to assume so, because his own military conviction has always been that such would have been the proper course. Whatever *coup de main* might have been possible against a harbor inadequately defended as were some of ours,—the fears of which, even, he considered exaggerated,—no serious operations against a defended seaboard were possible to any enemy after a transatlantic voyage, until recoaled. It would have been safe, militarily speaking, to place our two divisions before the ports named. It was safer to do so than to keep one at Hampton Roads; for offence is a safer course than defence.

[159] Consider the conditions. The Spaniards, after crossing the Atlantic, would have to coal. There were four principal ports at which they might do so,—Havana, Cienfuegos, Santiago, and San Juan de Puerto Rico. The first two, on the assumption, would be closed to them, unless they chose to fight a division so nearly equal to their own force that, whatever the result of the battle, the question of coaling would have possessed no further immediate interest for them. Santiago and San Juan, and any other suitable eastern port open to them—if such there was—were simply so many special instances of a particular case; and of these San Juan was the most favorable to them, because, being the most distant, it ensured more time for coaling and getting away again before our divisions could arrive. After their departure from Curaçao was known, but not their subsequent intentions, and while our divisions were proceeding to Havana and Cienfuegos, measures were under consideration at the Navy Department which would have made it even then difficult for them to escape action, if they went to San Juan for coal; but which would have raised the difficult close to the point of the impossible, [160] had our divisions from the first been placed before Havana and Cienfuegos, which strategic conditions dictated, but fears for our own inadequately defended coast prevented.

To ensure this result, the contemplated method, one simply of sustained readiness, was as follows. Adequate lookouts around Puerto Rico were to be stationed, by whom the enemy's approach would be detected and quickly cabled; and our two divisions were to be kept ready to proceed at an instant's notice, coaled to their best steaming lines, as far as this was compatible with a sufficiency of fuel to hold their ground after arriving off San Juan. Two of our fastest despatch vessels, likewise at their best steaming immersion, were to be held at Key West ready to start at once for Cienfuegos to notify the squadron there; two, in order that if one broke down on the way, one would surely arrive within twenty-four hours. Thus planned, the receipt of a cable at the Department from one of the lookouts off Puerto Rico would be like the touching of a button. The Havana division, reached within six hours, would start at once; that at Cienfuegos eighteen hours after the former. Barring [161] accidents, we should, in five days after the enemy's arrival, have had off San Juan the conditions which it took over a week to establish at Santiago; but, allowing for accidents, there would, within five days, have been at least one division, a force sufficient to hold the enemy in check.

Five days, it may be said, is not soon enough. It would have been quite soon enough in the case of Spaniards after a sea voyage of twenty-five hundred miles, in which the larger vessels had to share their coal with the torpedo destroyers. In case of a quicker enemy of more executive despatch, and granting, which will be rare, that a fleet's readiness to depart will be conditioned only by coal, and not by necessary engine repairs to some one vessel, it is to be remarked that the speed which can be, and has been, assumed for our ships in this particular case, nine knots, is far less than the most modest demands for a battleship,—such as those made even by the present writer, who is far from an advocate of extreme speed. Had not our deficiency of dry docks left our ships very foul, they could have covered the distance well within four days. Ships steady [162] at thirteen knots would have needed little over three; and it is *sustained* speed like this, not a spurt of eighteen knots for twelve hours, that is wanted. No one, however, need be at pains to dispute that circumstances alter cases; or that the promptness and executive ability of an enemy are very material circumstances. Similarly, although the method proposed would have had probable success at San Juan, and almost certain success at any shorter distance, it would at two thousand miles be very doubtfully expedient.

Assuming, moreover, that it had been thought unadvisable to move against San Juan, because doubtful of arriving in time, what would have been the situation had Cervera reached there, our armored divisions being off Havana and Cienfuegos? He would have been watched by the four lookouts—which were ordered before Santiago immediately upon his arrival there—and by them followed when he quitted port. Four leaves a good margin for detaching successively to cable ports before giving up this following game, and by that time his intentions would be apparent. Where, indeed, should he go? [163] Before Havana and Cienfuegos would be divisions capable of fighting him. Santiago, or any eastern port, is San Juan over again, with disadvantage of distance. Matanzas is but Havana; he would find himself anticipated there, because one of those vessels dogging his path would have hurried on to announce his approach. Were his destination, however, evidently a North Atlantic port, as some among us had fondly feared, our division before Havana would be recalled by cable, and that before Cienfuegos drawn back to Havana, leaving, of course, lookouts before the southern port. Cienfuegos is thereby uncovered, doubtless; but either the Spaniard fails to get there, not knowing our movements, or, if he rightly divines them and turns back, our coast is saved.

Strategy is a game of wits, with many unknown quantities; as Napoleon and Nelson have said—and not they alone—the unforeseen and chance must always be allowed for. But, if there are in it no absolute certainties, there are practical certainties, raised by experience to maxims, reasonable observance of which gives long odds. Prominent among [164] these certainties are the value of the offensive over the defensive, the advantage of a central position, and of interior lines. All these would have been united, strategically, by placing our armored divisions before Havana and Cienfuegos. As an offensive step, this supported, beyond any chance of defeat, the blockade of the Cuban coast, as proclaimed, with the incidental additional advantage that Key West, our base, was not only accessible to us, but defended against serious attack, by the mere situation of our Havana squadron. Central position and interior lines were maintained, for, Havana being nearly equidistant from Puerto Rico and the Chesapeake, the squadrons could be moved in the shortest time in either direction, and they covered all points of offence and defence within the limits of the theatre of war by lines shorter than those open to the enemy, which is what "interior lines" practically means.

If this disposition did possess these advantages, the question naturally arises whether it was expedient for the Havana division, before Cervera's arrival was known, and with the Flying Squadron still at Hampton Roads, to move to the eastward to San Juan, as was done. The [165] motive of this step, in which the Navy Department acquiesced, was the probability, which must be fully admitted, that San Juan was Cervera's primary destination. If it so proved, our squadron would be nearer at hand. It was likely, of course, that Cervera would first communicate with a neutral port, as he did at Martinique, to learn if the coast were clear before pushing for San Juan. The result of his going to the latter place would have been to present the strategic problem already discussed.

Cervera heard that our fleet was at San Juan, went to Curaçao, and afterwards to Santiago, because, as the Spanish Minister of Marine declared in the Cortes, it was the only port to which he could go. Our Admiral's official report, summing up the conditions after the bombardment of San Juan, as they suggested themselves to his mind at the time, has been quoted in a previous section. In the present we have sought to trace as vividly as possible the hurried and various measures consequent upon Cervera's movements; to reproduce, if may be, the perplexities—the anxieties, perhaps, but certainly not the apprehensions—of the next ten days, in which, though we did not [166] fear being beaten, we did fear being outwitted, which is to no man agreeable.

If Sampson's division had been before Havana and Schley's at Hampton Roads when Cervera appeared, the latter could have entered San Juan undisturbed. What could we then have done? In virtue of our central position, three courses were open. 1. We could have sent our Havana division to San Juan, as before proposed, and the Flying Squadron direct to the same point, with the disadvantage, however, as compared with the disposition advocated last, that the distance to it from Hampton Roads is four hundred miles more than from Cienfuegos. 2. We could have moved the Havana Squadron to San Juan, sending the Flying Squadron to Key West to coal and await further orders. This is only a modification of No. 1. Or, 3, we could have ordered the Flying Squadron to Key West, and at the same moment sent the Havana division before Cienfuegos,—a simultaneous movement which would have effected a great economy of time, yet involved no risk, owing to the distance of the Spanish division from the centre of operations.

[167] Of these three measures the last would have commended itself to the writer had Cervera's appearance, reported at Martinique, left it at all doubtful whether or not he were aiming for Havana or Cienfuegos. In our estimation, that was the strategic centre, and therefore to be covered before all else. So long as Cervera's destination was unknown, and might, however improbable, be our coast, there was possible justification for keeping the Flying Squadron there; the instant he was known to be in the West Indies, to close the two Cuban ports became the prime necessity. But had he entered San Juan without previous appearance, the first or the second should have been adopted, in accordance with the sound general principle that the enemy's fleet, if it probably can be reached, is the objective paramount to all others; because the control of the sea, by reducing the enemy's navy, is the determining consideration in a naval war.

Without dogmatizing, however, upon a situation which did not obtain, it appears now to the writer, not only that the eastward voyage of our Havana division was unfortunate, viewed in the light of subsequent events, but [168] that it should have been seen beforehand to be a mistake because inconsistent with a well-founded and generally accepted principle of war, the non-observance of which was not commanded by the conditions. The principle is that which condemns "eccentric" movements. The secondary definition of this word—"odd" or "peculiar"—has so dislodged all other meanings in common speech that it seems necessary to recall that primarily, by derivation, it signifies "away from the centre," to which sense it is confined in technical military phrase. Our centre of operations had been fixed, and rightly fixed, at Havana and Cienfuegos. It was subject, properly, to change—instant change—when the enemy's fleet was known to be within striking distance; but to leave the centre otherwise, on a calculation of probabilities however plausible, was a proposition that should have been squarely confronted with the principle, which itself is only the concrete expression of many past experiences. It is far from the writer's wish to advocate slavery to rule; no bondage is more hopeless or more crushing; but when one thinks of acting contrary to the weight of experience, the reasons [169] for such action should be most closely scrutinized, and their preponderance in the particular case determined.

These remarks are offered with no view of empty criticism of a mistake—if such it were—in which the writer was not without his share. In military judgments error is not necessarily censurable. One of the greatest captains has said: "The general who has made no mistake has made few campaigns." There are mistakes and mistakes; errors of judgment, such as the most capable man makes in the course of a life, and errors of conduct which demonstrate essential unfitness for office. Of the latter class was that of Admiral Byng, when he retired from Minorca; a weakness not unparalleled in later times, but which, whatever the indulgence accorded to the offender, is a military sin that should for itself receive no condonement of judgment. As instances of the former, both Nelson and Napoleon admitted, to quote the latter's words: "I have been so often mistaken that I no longer blush for it. " My wish is to illustrate, by a recent particular instance, a lesson professionally useful to the future,—the value of rules. By the disregard [170] of rule in this case we uncovered both Havana and Cienfuegos, which it was our object to close to the enemy's division. Had the latter been more efficient, he could have reached one or the other before we regained the centre. Our movement was contrary to rule; and while the inferences upon which it was based were plausible, they were not, in the writer's judgment, adequate to constitute the exception.

FOOTNOTES:

[3] The distance from Hampton Roads to Key West is increased, owing to the adverse current of the Gulf Stream through much of the route.

V ToC

The Guard Set Over Cervera.—Influence of Inadequate Numbers Upon the Conduct of Naval and Military Operations.—Cámara's Rush through the Mediterranean, and Consequent Measures taken by the United States.

The result of the various movements so far narrated was to leave the Flying Squadron May 22nd, off Cienfuegos, and Admiral Sampson's division off Havana, on the 21st. The latter was seriously diminished in mobile combatant force by the removal of the *Iowa*, detached to the south of the island to join the ships under Schley. It was confidently [171] expected that there, rather than at any northern port, the enemy would make his first appearance; and for that reason the Flying Squadron was strengthened by, and that off Havana deprived of, a vessel whose qualities would tell heavily in conflict with an active antagonist, such as a body of armored cruisers ought to be. Only by great good fortune could it be expected that the monitors, upon which Sampson for the moment had largely to depend, could impose an engagement upon Cervera's division if the latter sought to enter Havana by a dash. By taking from the Admiral his most powerful vessel, he was exposed to the mortification of seeing the enemy slip by and show his heels to our sluggish, low-freeboard, turreted vessels; but the solution was the best that could be reached under the conditions. It was not till the 28th of the month that the junction of the *Oregon* put our division before Havana on terms approaching equality as regards quickness of movement.

On the 19th of May the Department received probable, but not certain, information that the enemy's division had entered Santiago. This, as is now known, had occurred on the early [172] morning of the same day. Singularly enough, less than twenty-four hours before, on the 18th, the auxiliary steamer *St. Louis*, Captain Goodrich, lately one of the American Transatlantic liners, had been close in with the mouth of this port, which had hitherto lain outside our sphere of operations, and had made a determined and successful attempt to cut the telegraph cable leading from Santiago to Jamaica. In doing this, the *St. Louis*, which, like her sister ships (except the *St. Paul*), had not yet received an armament suitable to her size or duties, lay for three-quarters of an hour under the fire of the enemy, at a distance of little over a mile. Fortunately a six-inch rifled gun on the Socapa battery, which was then being mounted, was not ready until the following day; and the *St. Louis* held her ground without injury until a piece had been cut out of the cable. In this work she was assisted by the tug *Wompatuck*, Lieutenant-Commander Jungen. The two vessels then moved away to Guantanamo Bay, having been off Santiago nearly forty-eight hours. It may certainly be charged as good luck to Cervera that their departure before his arrival kept our Government long in [173] uncertainty as to the fact, which we needed to know in the most positive manner before stripping the Havana blockade in order to concentrate at Santiago. The writer remembers that the captain of the *St. Louis*, having soon afterwards to come north for coal, found it difficult to believe that he could have missed the Spanish vessels by so little; and the more so because he had spent the 19th off Guantanamo, less than fifty miles distant. By that time, however, our information, though still less than eye-witness, was so far probable as to preponderate over his doubts; but much perplexity would have been spared us had the enemy been seen by this ship, whose great speed would have brought immediate positive intelligence that all, and not only a part, had entered the port. On this point we did not obtain certainty until three weeks later.

In yet another respect luck, as it is commonly called, went against us at this time. The *Wompatuck* was sent by Captain Goodrich into the mouth of the harbor at Guantanamo to attempt to grapple the cable there. The tug and the *St. Louis* were both forced to retire, not by the weight of fire from the coast, [174] but by a petty Spanish gunboat, aided by "a small gun on shore." Could this fact have been communicated to Commodore Schley when he decided to return to Key West on the 26th, on account of the difficulty of coaling, he might have seen the facility with which the place could be secured and utilized for a coaling station, as it subsequently was by Admiral Sampson, and that there thus was no necessity of starting back some seven hundred miles to Key West, when he had with him four thousand tons of coal in a collier. When the lower bay was occupied, on the 8th of June, our attacking vessels were only the naval unprotected cruiser *Marblehead* and the auxiliary cruiser *Yankee*, the former of which was with the Flying Squadron during its passage from Cienfuegos to Santiago, and throughout the subsequent proceedings up to Sampson's arrival off the latter port. No resistance to them was made by the Spanish gunboat, before which the vulnerable and inadequately armed *St. Louis* and *Wompatuck* had very properly retired.

Although the information received of Cervera's entering Santiago was not reliable [175] enough to justify detaching Sampson's ships from before Havana, it was probable to a degree that made it imperative to watch the port in force at once. Telegrams were immediately sent out to assemble the four auxiliary cruisers—*St. Paul, St. Louis, Harvard,* and *Yale*—and the fast naval cruiser *Minneapolis* before the mouth of the harbor. The number of these ships shows the importance attached to the duty. It was necessary to allow largely for the chapter of accidents; for, to apply a pithy saying of the Chief of the Naval Bureau of Equipment,—"the only way to have coal enough is to have too much,"—the only way to assemble ships enough when things grow critical, is to send more than barely enough. All those that received their orders proceeded as rapidly as their conditions allowed, but the Department could not get hold of the *St. Louis*. This failure illustrates strongly the remark before made concerning the importance of knowing just where cruisers are to be found; for of all the five ships thus sought to be gathered, the *St. Louis* was, at the moment, the most important, through her experience of the defenceless state of the harbor at Guantanamo, [176] which she could have communicated to Schley. The latter, when he arrived off Santiago on the evening of the 26th, found the *Minneapolis*, the *St. Paul*, and the *Yale* on the ground. The *Harvard* had already been there, but had gone for the moment to St. Nicolas Mole, with despatches that the Commodore had sent before him from Cienfuegos. She joined the squadron again early next day, May 27th.

On the morning of the 25th, the *St. Paul* had captured the British steamer *Restormel*, with 2,400 tons of coal for the Spanish squadron. This vessel had gone first to Puerto Rico, and from there had been directed to Curaçao, where she arrived two days after Cervera had departed. When taken she reported that two other colliers were in Puerto Rico when she sailed thence. This would seem to indicate that that port, and not Santiago, had been the original destination of the enemy, for it would have been quite as easy for the colliers to go to Santiago at once; probably safer, for we were not then thinking of Santiago in comparison with San Juan. This conjecture is strengthened by the fact that there were only 2,300 tons of Cardiff coal in Santiago, a condition which [177] shows both how little the Spanish Government expected to use the port and how serious this capture at this instant was to the enemy.

The intention of Commodore Schley to return to Key West precipitated the movement of Admiral Sampson, with his two fastest ships, to Santiago; but the step would certainly have been taken as soon as the doubt whether all the Spanish division had entered was removed. The Department, under its growing conviction that the enemy was there, had already been increasingly disturbed by the delay of the Flying Squadron before Cienfuegos. This delay was due to the uncertainty of its commander as to whether or not Cervera was in the latter port; nor was there then known reason to censure the decision of the officer on the spot, whose information, dependent upon despatch vessels, or upon local scouting, was necessarily, in some respects, more meagre than that of the Department, in cable communication with many quarters. Nevertheless, he was mistaken, and each succeeding hour made the mistake more palpable and more serious to those in Washington; not, indeed, that demonstrative proof had been received there—far from it—but there was [178] that degree of reasonable probability which justifies practical action in all life, and especially in war. There was not certainty enough to draw away our ships from before Havana,—to the exposure also of Key West,—but there was quite sufficient certainty to take the chance of leaving Cienfuegos and going off Santiago; for, to put the case at its weakest, we could not close both ports, and had, therefore, to make a choice. Against the risk of the enemy trying to dash out of Santiago and run for some other point, provision was made by a telegram to the *Yale* to inform every vessel off Santiago that the Flying Squadron was off Cienfuegos, and that orders had been sent it to proceed with all possible despatch off Santiago. If, therefore, the enemy did run out before the arrival of Schley, our scouts would know where to look for the latter; that is, somewhere on the shortest line between the two ports.

The embarrassment imposed upon the Department, under the telegram that the Flying Squadron was returning to Key West, was increased greatly by the fact that the five cruisers ordered before the port were getting very short of coal. If the squadron held its ground, this [179] was comparatively immaterial. It would be injurious, unquestionably, to the communications and to the lookout, but not necessarily fatal to the object in view, which was that Cervera should not get out without a fight and slip away again into the unknown. But, if the squadron went, the cruisers could not stay, and the enemy might escape unobserved. Fortunately, on second thoughts, the Commodore decided to remain; but before that was known to the Department, Sampson had been directed, on May 29th, to proceed with the *New York* and the *Oregon*, the latter of which had only joined him on the 28th. The telegram announcing that the Flying Squadron would hold on came indeed before the two ships started, but it was not thought expedient to change their orders. Word also had then been received that two of the Spanish division had been sighted inside from our own vessels, and though this still left a doubt as to the whereabouts of the others, it removed the necessity of covering Key West, which had caused the Department, on the first knowledge of Schley's returning, to limit its orders to Sampson to be ready to set out for Santiago the instant the Flying Squadron

[180] returned. By the departure of the *New York* and the *Oregon*, the *Indiana* was left the only battleship to the westward. Her speed was insufficient to keep up with the two others, and it was determined to employ her in convoying the army when it was ready,—a duty originally designed for Sampson's division as a whole.

Admiral Sampson with his two ships arrived off Santiago on the 1st of June at 6 A.M., and established at once the close watch of the port which lasted until the sally and destruction of Cervera's squadron. "From that time on," says the Spanish Lieutenant Muller, who was in the port from the first, as second in command of the naval forces of the province, "the hostile ships, which were afterwards increased in number, established day and night a constant watch, without withdrawing at nightfall, as they used to do." Into the particulars of this watch, which lasted for a month and which effectively prevented any attempt of the enemy to go out by night, the writer does not purpose to enter, as his object in this series of papers is rather to elicit the general lessons derivable from the war than to give the details of particular operations. It is only just to say, however, that all the [181] dispositions of the blockade,—to use the common, but not strictly accurate, expression,—from the beginning of June to the day of the battle, were prescribed by the commander-in-chief on the spot, without controlling orders, and with little, if any, suggestion on the subject from the Department. The writer remembers none; but he does well remember the interest with which, during the dark nights of the month, he watched the size of the moon, which was new on the 18th, and the anxiety each morning lest news might be received of a successful attempt to get away on the part of the enemy, whose reputed speed so far exceeded that of most of our ships. It was not then known that, by reason of the methods unremittingly enforced by our squadron, it was harder to escape from Santiago by night than by day, because of the difficulty of steering a ship through an extremely narrow channel, with the beam of an electric light shining straight in the eyes, as would there have been the case for a mile before reaching the harbor's mouth.

The history of the time—now nearly a year—that has elapsed since these lines were first written, impels the author, speaking as a [182] careful student of the naval operations that have illustrated the past two centuries and a half, to say that in his judgment no more onerous and important duty than the guard off Santiago fell upon any officer of the United States during the hostilities; and that the judgment, energy, and watchfulness with which it was fulfilled by Admiral Sampson merits the highest praise. The lack of widely diffused popular appreciation of military conditions, before referred to in these papers, has been in nothing more manifest than in the failure to recognize generally, and by suitable national reward, both the difficulty of his task, and that the dispositions maintained by him ensured the impossibility of Cervera's escaping undetected, as well as the success of the action which followed his attempt at flight. This made further fighting on Spain's part hopeless and vindicated, if vindication were needed, the Department's choice of the commander-in-chief; but, as a matter of fact, the reply of that great admiral and experienced administrator, Lord St. Vincent, when he sent Nelson to the Nile, meets decisively all such cases: "Those who are responsible for results"—as [183] the Navy Department (under the President), was—"must be allowed the choice of their agents." The writer may perhaps be excused for adding, that, having had no share, direct or indirect, in this selection, which entirely preceded his connection with the Department, he can have no motive of self-justification regarding an appointment for which he could deserve neither credit nor blame.

The office of the Navy Department at that moment, so far as Santiago itself was concerned, was chiefly administrative: to maintain the number of ships and their necessary supplies of coal, ammunition, and healthy food at the highest point consistent with the requirements of other parts of the field of war. During the month of June, being, as it was, the really decisive period of the campaign, these demands for increase of force naturally rose higher in every quarter. A numerous convoy had to be provided for the army expedition; the battle fleet had to be supplemented with several light cruisers; it became evident that the sphere of the blockade must be extended, which meant many more ships; and in the midst of all this, Cámara started for Suez. All this only instances the [184] common saying, "It never rains but it pours." Our battle fleet before Santiago was more than powerful enough to crush the hostile squadron in a very short time, if the latter attempted a stand-up fight. The fact was so evident that it was perfectly clear nothing of the kind would be hazarded; but, nevertheless, we could not afford to diminish the number of armored vessels on this spot, now become the determining centre of the conflict. The possibility of the situation was twofold. Either the enemy might succeed in an effort at evasion, a chance which required us to maintain a distinctly superior force of battleships in order to allow the occasional absence of one or two for coaling or repairs, besides as many lighter cruisers as could be mustered for purposes of lookout, or, by merely remaining quietly at anchor, protected from attack by the lines of torpedoes, he might protract a situation which tended not only to wear out our ships, but also to keep them there into the hurricane season,—a risk which was not, perhaps, adequately realized by the people of the United States.

It is desirable at this point to present certain other elements of the naval situation which [185] weightily affected naval action at the moment, and which, also, were probably overlooked by the nation at large, for they give a concrete illustration of conditions which ought to influence our national policy, as regards the navy, in the present and immediate future. We had to economize our ships because they were too few. There was no reserve. The Navy Department had throughout, and especially at this period, to keep in mind, not merely the exigencies at Santiago, but the fact that we had not a battleship in the home ports that could in six months be made ready to replace one lost or seriously disabled, as the *Massachusetts*, for instance, not long afterwards was, by running on an obstruction in New York Bay. Surprise approaching disdain was expressed, both before and after the destruction of Cervera's squadron, that the battle fleet was not sent into Santiago either to grapple the enemy's ships there, or to support the operations of the army, in the same way, for instance, that Farragut crossed the torpedo lines at Mobile. The reply—and, in the writer's judgment, the more than adequate reason—was that the country could not at that time, under the political conditions which [186] then obtained, afford to risk the loss or disablement of a single battleship, unless the enterprise in which it was hazarded carried a reasonable probability of equal or greater loss to the enemy, leaving us, therefore, as strong as before relatively to the naval power which in the course of events might yet be arrayed against us. If we lost ten thousand men, the country could replace them; if we lost a battleship, it could not be replaced. The issue of the war, as a whole and in every locality to which it extended, depended upon naval force, and it was imperative to achieve, not success only, but success delayed no longer than necessary. A million of the best soldiers would have been powerless in face of hostile control of the sea. Dewey had not a battleship, but there can be no doubt that that capable admiral thought he ought to have one or more; and so he ought, if we had had them to spare. The two monitors would be something, doubtless, when they arrived; but, like all their class, they lacked mobility.

When Cámara started by way of Suez for the East, it was no more evident than it was before that we ought to have battleships there. That [187] was perfectly plain from the beginning; but battleships no more than men can be in two places at once, and until Cámara's movement had passed beyond the chance of turning west, the Spanish fleet in the Peninsula had, as regarded the two fields of war, the West Indies and the Philippines, the recognized military advantage of an interior position. In accepting inferiority in the East, and concentrating our available force in the West Indies, thereby ensuring a superiority over any possible combination of Spanish vessels in the latter quarter, the Department acted rightly and in accordance with sound military precedent; but it must be remembered that the Spanish Navy was not the only possibility of the day. The writer was not in a position to know then, and does not know now, what weight the United States Government attached to the current rumors of possible political friction with other states whose people were notoriously sympathizers with our enemy. The public knows as much about that as he does; but it was clear that if a disposition to interfere did exist anywhere, it would not be lessened by a serious naval disaster to us, such as the loss of one of our few battleships would [188] be. Just as in the maintenance of a technically "effective" blockade of the Cuban ports, so, also, in sustaining the entireness and vigor of the battle fleet, the attitude of foreign Powers as well as the strength of the immediate enemy had to be considered. For such reasons it was recommended that the orders on this point to Admiral Sampson should be peremptory; not that any doubt existed as to the discretion of that officer, who justly characterized the proposition to throw the ships upon the mine fields of Santiago as suicidal folly, but because it was felt that the burden of such a decision should be assumed by a superior authority, less liable to suffer in personal reputation from the idle imputations of over-caution, which at times were ignorantly made by some who ought to have known better, but did not. "The matter is left to your discretion," the telegram read, "except that the United States armored vessels must not be risked."

When Cervera's squadron was once cornered, an intelligent opponent would, under any state of naval preparedness, have seen the advisability of forcing him out of the port by an attack in the rear, which could be made only by an army. [189] As Nelson said on one occasion, "What is wanted now is not more ships, but troops." Under few conditions should such a situation be prolonged. But the reasons adduced in the last paragraph made it doubly incumbent upon us to bring the matter speedily to an issue, and the combined expedition from Tampa was at once ordered. Having in view the number of hostile troops in the country surrounding Santiago, as shown by the subsequent returns of prisoners, and shrewdly suspected by ourselves beforehand, it was undoubtedly desirable to employ a larger force than was sent. The criticism made upon the inadequate number of troops engaged in this really daring movement is intrinsically sound, and would be wholly accurate if directed, not against the enterprise itself, but against the national shortsightedness which gave us so trivial an army at the outbreak of the war. The really hazardous nature of the movement is shown by the fact that the column of Escario, three thousand strong, from Manzanillo, reached Santiago on July 3rd; too late, it is true, abundantly too late, to take part in the defence of San Juan and El Caney, upon holding which the city depended for food and [190] water; yet not so late but that it gives a shivering suggestion how much more arduous would have been the task of our troops had Escario come up in time. The incident but adds another to history's long list of instances where desperate energy and economy of time have wrested safety out of the jaws of imminent disaster. The occasion was one that called upon us to take big risks; and success merely justifies doubly an attempt which, from the obvious balance of advantages and disadvantages, was antecedently justified by its necessity, and would not have been fair subject for blame, even had it failed.

The Navy Department did not, however, think that even a small chance of injury should be taken which could be avoided; and it may be remarked that, while the man is unfit for command who, on emergency, is unable to run a very great risk for the sake of decisive advantage, he, on the other hand, is only less culpable who takes even a small risk of serious harm against which reasonable precaution can provide. It has been well said that Nelson took more care of his topgallant masts, [4] in ordinary [191] cruising, than he did of his whole fleet when the enemy was to be checked or beaten; and this combination of qualities apparently opposed is found in all strong military characters to the perfection of which both are necessary. It was determined, accordingly, to collect for the transports a numerous naval guard or convoy, to secure them against possible attacks by the Spanish gunboats distributed along the north coast of Cuba, by which route the voyage was to be made. The care was probably thought excessive by many and capable men; but the unforeseen is ever happening in war. Here or there a young Spanish officer might unexpectedly prove, not merely brave, as they all are, but enterprising, which few of them seem to be. The transport fleet had no habit of manœuvring together; the captains, many of them, were without interest in the war, and with much interest in their owners, upon whom they commonly depended for employment; straggling, and panic in case of attack, could be surely predicted; and, finally, as we scarcely had men enough for the work before them, why incur the hazard of sacrificing even one ship-load of our most efficient but all too small [192] regular army? For such reasons it was decided to collect a dozen of the smaller cruisers, any one of which could handle a Spanish gunboat, and which, in virtue of their numbers, could be so distributed about the transports as to forestall attack at all points. The mere notoriety that so powerful a flotilla accompanied the movement was protection greater, perhaps, than the force itself; for it would impose quiescence even upon a more active enemy. As a further measure of precaution, directions were given to watch also the torpedo destroyer in San Juan during the passage of the army. The *Indiana*, as has been said, formed part of the convoy; the dispositions and order of sailing being arranged, and throughout superintended, by her commanding officer, Captain Henry C. Taylor.

On Saturday, June 4th, Commodore Remey, commanding the naval base at Key West, telegraphed that the naval vessels composing the convoy would be ready to sail that evening. The army was embarked and ready to move on the 8th, but early that morning was received the report, alluded to in a previous paper, that an armored cruiser with three vessels in [193] company had been sighted by one of our blockading fleet the evening before, in the Nicolas Channel, on the north coast of Cuba. Upon being referred back, the statement was confirmed by the officer making it, and also by another vessel which had passed over the same ground at nearly the same time. The account being thus both specific and positive, the sailing of the transports was countermanded,—the naval vessels of the convoy being sent out from Key West to scour the waters where the suspicious ships had been seen, and Admiral Sampson directed to send his two fastest armored vessels to Key West, in order that the expedition might proceed in force. The Admiral, being satisfied that the report was a mistake, of a character similar to others made to him at the same time, did not comply; a decision which, under the circumstances of his fuller knowledge, must be considered proper as well as fortunate. The incident was mortifying at the time, and—considering by how little Escario arrived late—might have been disastrous; but it is one of those in which it is difficult to assign blame, though easy to draw a very obvious moral for outlooks.

[194] The expedition finally got away from Tampa on the 14th of June, and arrived off Santiago on the 20th. The process of collecting and preparing the convoy, the voyage itself, and the delay caused by the false alarm, constituted together a period of three weeks, during which the naval vessels of the expedition were taken away from the blockade. Some days more were needed to coal them, and to get them again to their stations. Meanwhile it was becoming evident that the limits of the blockade must be extended, in order that full benefit might be derived from it as a military measure. The southern ports of Cuba west of Santiago, and especially the waters about the Isle of Pines and Batabano, which is in close rail connection with Havana, were receiving more numerous vessels, as was also the case with Sagua la Grande, on the north. In short, the demand for necessaries was producing an increasing supply, dependent upon Jamaica and Mexico in the south, upon Europe and North American ports in the north, and the whole was developing into a system which would go far to defeat our aims, unless counteracted by more widespread and closer-knit measures on [195] our part. It was decided, therefore, to proclaim a blockade of the south coast of Cuba from Cape Cruz, a little west of Santiago, to Cape Frances, where the foul ground west of the Isle of Pines terminates. The Isle of Pines itself was to be seized, in order to establish there a secure base, for coal and against hurricanes, for the small vessels which alone could operate in the surrounding shoal water; and an expedition, composed mainly of the battalion of marines, was actually on the way for that purpose when the protocol was signed. During the three weeks occupied by the preparation and passage of the Santiago expedition, the blockade had been barely "effective," technically; it could not at all be considered satisfactory from our point of view, although we were stripping the coast defence fleet of its cruisers, one by one, for the service in Cuba. Our utmost hope at the time, and with every available vessel we could muster, was so far to satisfy the claims of technicality, as to forestall any charges of ineffectiveness by neutrals, whose cruisers at times seemed somewhat curious.

In the midst of all this extra strain Cámara's squadron left Cadiz and made its hurried rush [196] eastward. One effect of this was to release, and instantly, all the patrol vessels on our northern coast. These were immediately ordered to Key West for blockade duty, Commodore Howell also going in person to take charge of this work. On the other hand, however, uneasiness could not but be felt for Dewey in case Cámara actually went on, for, except the monitor *Monterey*, we could get no armored ship out before the two Spanish armored vessels arrived; and if they had the same speed which they maintained to Suez—ten knots—it was doubtful whether the *Monterey* would anticipate them. It may be mentioned here, as an interesting coincidence, that the same day that word came that Cámara had started back for Spain, a telegram was also received that the *Monterey* had had to put back to Honolulu, for repairs to the collier which accompanied her. This, of course, was news then ten days old, communication from Honolulu to San Francisco being by steamer, not by cable.

The strengthening of our blockade by the vessels of the northern patrol fleet was therefore the first and, as it proved, the only lasting result of Cámara's move. What the object [197] was of that singular "vagabondaggio," as it is not inaptly called by an Italian critic, is to the author incomprehensible, to use also the qualifying word of the same foreign writer. That the intention was merely to provoke us to some "eccentric" movement, by playing upon our fears about our forces at Manila, would be perfectly reconcilable with going as far as Port Said, and remaining there for some days, as was done, in difficulty, actual or feigned, about getting coal; but why the large expense was incurred of passing through the canal, merely to double the amount by returning, is beyond understanding. It may have been simply to carry bluff to the extreme point; but it is difficult not to suspect some motive not yet revealed, and perhaps never to be known.

Possibly, however, the measures taken by ourselves may have had upon the Spanish Government the effect which, in part, they were intended to produce. A squadron of two battleships and four cruisers, drawn from Admiral Sampson's fleet, was constituted to go to Manila by way of Suez, under the command of Commodore Watson, until then in charge of the blockade on the north coast of [198] Cuba. Colliers to accompany these were at the same time prepared in our Atlantic ports. Upon the representations of the Admiral, he was authorized to suspend the sailing of the detachment until all the armored vessels were fully coaled, in order to ensure maintaining before Santiago for a considerable period the five that would be left to him. To this modification of the first order contributed also the darkness of the nights at that moment; for the moon, though growing, was still young. But, as our object was even more to prevent Cámara from proceeding than to send the reinforcement, it was desired that these dispositions should have full publicity, and, to ensure it the more fully, Watson was directed to go in all haste to Santiago with his flagship, the *Newark*, to take over his new command, the avowed objective of which was the Spanish coast, then deprived of much of its defence by the departure of Cámara's ships, and most imperfectly provided with local fortifications. Had Cámara gone on to the East, Watson would have followed him, and, although arriving later, there was no insuperable difficulty to so combining the movements of our two [199] divisions—Dewey's and Watson's—as to decide the final result, and to leave Spain without her second division of ships.

Cámara's delay at the Mediterranean end of the Canal, which extended over several days, suggested either doubts as to the reality of his rumored destination, or a belief that the equipment and preparation—in coal especially—for so distant an expedition had been imperfect. This contributed to postpone Watson's departure, and the first passage of the Canal (July 2nd) by the Spaniards coincided in date very closely with the destruction of their other division under Cervera. After the action off Santiago the battleships needed to be again supplied with ammunition, and before that could be effected Cámara was on his way back to Spain.

This abandonment by the enemy of their projected voyage to Manila concurred with the critical position of the army before Santiago to postpone the project of reinforcing Dewey, who no longer needed battleships so far as his immediate operations were concerned. Besides, the arrival of both the *Monterey* and the *Monadnock* was now assured, even if the enemy resumed his movement, which was scarcely [200] possible. When Santiago fell, however, it was felt to be necessary to re-establish our fleet in the Pacific, by way either of the Straits of Magellan or of the Suez Canal. The latter was chosen, and the entire battle fleet—except the *Texas*, rejected on account of her small coal endurance—was directed to join the movement and to accompany some distance within the straits the two battleships which, with their smaller cruisers and colliers, were to go to Manila. The preparations for this movement were kept secret for quite a time, under the cover of an avowed intention to proceed against Puerto Rico; but nothing, apparently, can wholly escape the prying curiosity of the Press, which dignifies this not always reputable quality with the title of "enterprise." No great harm resulted; possibly even the evident wish of the Government for secrecy, though thus betrayed, may have increased the apprehension of the enemy as to the damage intended to their coasts.

On the latter point the position of our Government, as understood by the writer, was perfectly simple. In case the enemy refused peace when resistance was obviously and utterly hopeless, bombardment of a seaport might be [201] resorted to, but with the utmost reluctance, and merely to compel submission and acquiescence in demonstrated facts. It is not possible to allow one's own people to be killed and their substance wasted merely because an adversary will not admit he is whipped, when he is. When our fleet reached the Spanish coast that case might have arisen; but probably the unwillingness of our Government so to act would have postponed its decision to the very last moment, in order to spare the enemy the final humiliation of yielding, not to reasonable acceptance of facts, but to direct threat of violence. The purpose of bombardment, so freely asserted by the Press, was one of the numerous baseless discoveries with which it enlightened its reader during the hostilities,—mixtures of truth and error, so ingeniously proportioned as to constitute an antidote, than which none better could then be had against its numerous indiscretions.

The determining factor in this proposed movement of the battle fleet as a whole was the necessity, or at least the advantage, of reinforcing Dewey, and of placing two battleships in the Pacific. It was not thought expedient now [202] to send them by themselves, as at first proposed, for the reason already given in another instance in this paper; that is, the impropriety of taking even a small risk, if unnecessary. Cámara's two ships had now returned to Spain, and there were besides in the ports of the Peninsula other armed vessels, which, though evidently unfit for a distant voyage, might be good for some work in the Straits of Gibraltar, where our two ships must pass. That the latter would beat them all, if assembled, we quite believed, as we had hoped that the *Oregon* might do had she met Cervera; but the *Oregon* could not be helped without neglecting more immediately pressing duties, whereas, at the end of July, there was nothing to detain our heavy ships in the West Indies. It was determined, therefore, to keep them massed and to send them across the ocean. It was probable, nearly to the extent of absolute certainty, that neither before nor after the separation of the division bound for the East would the entire Spanish Navy venture an attack upon the formidable force thus confronting its ports. To ensure success without fighting is always a proper object of military dispositions; and, [203] moreover, there were reasons before alluded to for maintaining in perfect integrity vessels whose organized fighting efficiency had now been fully vindicated to the world. Even during peace negotiations, one's position is not injured by the readiness of the battle fleet. In short, it should be an accepted apothegm, with those responsible for the conduct of military operations, that "War is business," to which actual fighting is incidental. As in all businesses, the true aim is the best results at the least cost; or, as the great French admiral, Tourville, said two centuries ago, "The best victories are those which expend least of blood, of hemp, and of iron." Such results, it is true, are more often granted to intelligent daring than to excessive caution; but no general rule can supersede the individual judgment upon the conditions before it. There are no specifics in warfare.

To this main reason, others less immediately important concurred. The ships would be taken out of a trying climate, and removed from the chance of hurricanes; while the crews would receive a benefit, the value of which is avouched by naval history, in change of scene, of occupation, and of interests. The possibility [204] of the enemy attempting to divert us from our aim, by sending vessels to the West Indies, was considered, and, although regarded as wildly improbable, provision against it was made. As Nelson wrote to his commander-in-chief before the advance on Copenhagen: "There are those who think, if you leave the Sound open, that the Danish fleet may sail from Copenhagen to join the Dutch or French. I own I have no fears on that subject; for it is not likely that whilst their capital is menaced with an attack, nine thousand of her best men should be sent out of the kingdom." It was still less probable that Spain in the present case would attempt any diversion to the West Indies, and the movement of our heavy-armored vessels to her shores could now justly be considered to cover all our operations on this side of the Atlantic. The detailed arrangements made for frequent communication, however, would have kept the Department practically in touch with our fleet throughout, and have enabled us to counteract any despairing effort of the enemy.

FOOTNOTES:

[4] The lighter upper masts, upon which speed much depended in moderate weather.

[205]

THE PEACE CONFERENCE AND THE MORAL ASPECT OF WAR

[206]
[207]

THE PEACE CONFERENCE AND THE MORAL ASPECT OF WAR ToC

To determine the consequences of an historical episode, such as the recent Peace Conference at The Hague, is not a matter for prophecy, but for experience, which alone can decide what positive issues, for good or for ill, shall hereafter trace their source to this beginning. The most that the present can do is to take note of the point so far reached, and of apparent tendencies manifested; to seek for the latter a right direction; to guide, where it can, currents of general thought, the outcome of which will be beneficial or injurious, according as their course is governed by a just appreciation of fundamental truths.

The calling of the Conference of The Hague originated in an avowed desire to obtain relief from immediate economical burdens, by the adoption of some agreement to restrict the [208] preparations for war, and the consequent expense involved in national armaments; but before its meeting the hope of disarmament had fallen into the background, the vacant place being taken by the project of abating the remoter evils of recurrent warfare, by giving a further impulse, and a more clearly defined application, to the principle of arbitration, which thenceforth assumed pre-eminence in the councils of the Conference. This may be considered the point at which we have arrived. The assembled representatives of many nations, including all the greatest upon the earth, have decided that it is to arbitration men must look for relief, rather than to partial disarmament, or even to an arrest in the progress of preparations for war. Of the beneficence of the practice of arbitration, of the wisdom of substituting it, when possible, for the appeal to arms, with all the misery therefrom resulting, there can be no doubt; but it will be expected that in its application, and in its attempted development, the tendencies of the day, both good and bad, will make themselves felt. If, on the one hand, there is solid ground for rejoicing in the growing inclination to resort [209] first to an impartial arbiter, if such can be found, when occasion for collision arises, there is, on the other hand, cause for serious reflection when this most humane impulse is seen to favor methods, which by compulsion shall vitally impair the moral freedom, and the consequent moral responsibility, which are the distinguishing glory of the rational man, and of the sovereign state.

One of the most unfortunate characteristics of our present age is the disposition to impose by legislative enactment—by external compulsion, that is—restrictions of a moral character, which are either fundamentally unjust, or at least do not carry with them the moral sense of the community, as a whole. It is not religious faith alone that in the past has sought to propagate itself by force of law, which ultimately is force of physical coercion. If the religious liberty of the individual has been at last won, as we hope forever, it is sufficiently notorious that the propensity of majorities to control the freedom of minorities, in matters of disputed right and wrong, still exists, as certain and as tyrannical as ever was the will of Philip II. that there should be no heretic [210] within his dominion. Many cannot so much as comprehend the thought of the English Bishop, that it was better to see England free than England sober.

In matters internal to a state, the bare existence of a law imposes an obligation upon the individual citizen, whatever his personal conviction of its rightfulness or its wisdom. Yet is such obligation not absolute. The primary duty, attested alike by the law and the gospel, is submission. The presumption is in favor of the law; and if there lie against it just cause for accusation, on the score either of justice or of expediency, the interests of the Commonwealth and the precepts of religion alike demand that opposition shall be conducted according to the methods, and within the limits, which the law of the land itself prescribes. But it may be—it has been, and yet again may be—that the law, however regular in its enactment, and therefore unquestionable on the score of formal authority, either outrages fundamental political right, or violates the moral dictates of the individual conscience. Of the former may be cited as an instance the Stamp Act, perfectly regular as regarded statutory validity, which [211] kindled the flame of revolution in America. Of the second, the Fugitive Slave Law, within the memory of many yet living, is a conspicuous illustration. Under such conditions, the moral right of resistance is conceded—nay, is affirmed and emphasized—by the moral consciousness of the races from which the most part of the American people have their origin, and to which, almost wholly, we owe our political and religious traditions. Such resistance may be passive, accepting meekly the penalty for disobedience, as the martyr who for conscience' sake refused the political requirement of sacrificing to the image of the Cæsar; or it may be active and violent, as when our forefathers repelled taxation without representation, or when men and women, of a generation not yet wholly passed away, refused to violate their consciences by acquiescing in the return of a slave to his bondage, resorting to evasion or to violence, according to their conditions or temperaments, but in every case deriving the sanction for their unlawful action from the mandate of their personal conscience.

And let it be carefully kept in mind that it is not the absolute right or wrong of the [212] particular act, as seen in the clearer light of a later day, that justified men, whether in the particular instances cited, or in other noteworthy incidents in the long series of steps by which the English-speaking races have ascended to their present political development. It is not the demonstrable rightfulness of a particular action, as seen in the dispassionate light of the arbiter, posterity, that has chiefly constituted the merit of the individual rebel against the law in which he beheld iniquity; the saving salt, which has preserved the healthfulness of the body politic, has been the fidelity to Conscience, to the faithful, if passionate, arbiter of the moment, whose glorious predominance in the individual or in the nation gives a better assurance of the highest life than does the clearest intellectual perception of the rightfulness, or of the expediency, of a particular course. One may now see, or think that he sees, as does the writer, with Lincoln, that if slavery is not wrong, nothing is wrong. It was not so clear half a century ago; and while no honor is too great for those early heroes, who for this sublime conviction withstood obloquy and persecution, legal and illegal, it should be [213] never forgotten that the then slave States, in their resolute determination to maintain, by arms, if need be, and against superior force, that which they believed to be their constitutional political right, made no small contribution to the record of fidelity to conscience and to duty, which is the highest title of a nation to honor. Be it by action or be it by submission, by action positive or by action negative, whatsoever is not of faith—of conviction—is sin.

The just and necessary exaltation of the law as the guarantee of true liberty, with the consequent accepted submission of the individual to it, and the recognized presumption in favor of such submission, have tended to blind us to the fact that the individual, in our highest consciousness, has never surrendered his moral freedom,—his independence of conscience. No human law overbears that supreme appeal, which carries the matter from the tribunal of man into the presence of God; nor can human law be pleaded at this bar as the excuse for a violation of conscience. It is a dangerous doctrine, doubtless, to preach that there may be a "higher law" than obedience to law; but truth is not to be rejected because dangerous, and the [214] time is not long past when the phrase voiced a conviction, the forcible assertion of which brought slavery to an end forever.

The resort to arms by a nation, when right cannot otherwise be enforced, corresponds, or should correspond, precisely to the acts of the individual man which have been cited; for the old conception of an appeal to the Almighty, resembling in principle the mediæval trial by battle, is at best but a partial view of the truth, seen from one side only. However the result may afterwards be interpreted as indicative of the justice of a cause,—an interpretation always questionable,—a state, when it goes to war, should do so not to test the rightfulness of its claims, but because, being convinced in its conscience of that rightfulness, no other means of overcoming evil remains.

Nations, like men, have a conscience. Like men, too, the light of conscience is in nations often clouded, or misguided, by passion or by interest. But what of that? Does a man discard his allegiance to conscience because he knows that, itself in harmony with right, its message to him is perplexed and obscured by his own infirmities? Not so. Fidelity to [215] conscience implies not only obedience to its dictates, but earnest heart-searching, the use of every means, to ascertain its true command; yet withal, whatever the mistrust of the message, the supremacy of the conscience is not impeached. When it is recognized that its final word is spoken, nothing remains but obedience. Even if mistaken, the moral wrong of acting against conviction works a deeper injury to the man, and to his kind, than can the merely material disasters that may follow upon obedience. Even the material evils of war are less than the moral evil of compliance with wrong.

"Yes, my friend," replied to me a foreign diplomatist to whom I was saying some such things, "but remember that only a few years ago the conscience of your people was pressing you into war with Great Britain in the Venezuelan question." "Admitting," I replied, "that the first national impulse, the first movement of the conscience, if you like, was mistaken,—which is at least open to argument,—it remains that there was no war; time for deliberation was taken, and more than that can be asked of no conscience, national or personal. [216] But, further, had the final decision of conscience been that just cause for war existed, no evil that war brings could equal the moral declension which a nation inflicts upon itself, and upon mankind, by deliberate acquiescence in wrong, which it recognizes and which it might right." Nor is this conclusion vitiated by the fact that war is made at times upon mistaken conviction. It is not the accuracy of the decision, but the faithfulness to conviction, that constitutes the moral worth of an action, national or individual.

The general consciousness of this truth is witnessed by a common phrase, which excludes from suggested schemes of arbitration all questions which involve "national honor or vital interests." No one thing struck me more forcibly during the Conference at The Hague than the exception taken and expressed, although in a very few quarters, to the word "honor," in this connection. There is for this good reason; for the word, admirable in itself and if rightly understood, has lost materially in the clearness of its image and superscription, by much handling and by some misapplication. Honor does not forbid a nation to acknowledge that it is [217] wrong, or to recede from a step which it has taken through wrong motives or mistaken reasons; yet it has at times been so thought, to the grievous injury of the conception of honor. It is not honor, necessarily, but sound policy, which prescribes that peace with a semi-civilized foe should not be made after a defeat; but, however justifiable the policy, the word "honor" is defaced by thus misapplying it.

The varying fortunes, the ups and downs of the idea of arbitration at the Conference of The Hague, as far as my intelligence could follow them, produced in me two principal conclusions, which so far confirmed my previous points of view that I think I may now fairly claim for them that they have ripened into *opinions*, between which word, and the cruder, looser views received passively as *impressions*, I have been ever careful to mark a distinction. In the first place, compulsory arbitration stands at present no chance of general acceptance. There is but one way as yet in which arbitration can be compulsory; for the dream of some advanced thinkers, of an International Army, charged with imposing the decrees of an International Tribunal upon [218] a recalcitrant state, may be dismissed as being outside of practical international politics, until at least the nations are ready for the intermediate step of moral compulsion, imposed by a self-assumed obligation—by a promise. Compulsory arbitration as yet means only the moral compulsion of a pledge, taken beforehand, and more or less comprehensive, to submit to arbitration questions which rest still in the unknown future; the very terms of which therefore cannot be foreseen. Although there is a certain active current of agitation in favor of such stipulations, there is no general disposition of governments to accede, except under very narrow and precise limitations, and in questions of less than secondary importance.

Secondly, there appears to be, on the other hand, a much greater disposition than formerly to entertain favorably the idea of arbitration, as a means to be in all cases considered, and where possible to be adopted, in order to solve peaceably difficulties which threaten peace. In short, the consciences of the nations are awake to the wickedness of unnecessary war, and are disposed, as a general rule, to seek first, and where admissible, the counterpoise [219] of an impartial judge, where such can be found, to correct the bias of national self-will; but there is an absolute indisposition, an instinctive revolt, against signing away, beforehand, the national conscience, by a promise that any other arbiter than itself shall be accepted in questions of the future, the import of which cannot yet be discerned. Of this feeling the vague and somewhat clumsy phrase, "national honor and vital interests," has in the past been the expression; for its very indeterminateness reserved to conscience in every case the decision,—"May another judge for me here, or must I be bound by my own sense of right?"

Under these circumstances, and having reached so momentous a stage in progress as is indicated by the very calling together of a world conference for the better assuring of peace, may it not be well for us to pause a moment and take full account of the idea, Arbitration, on the right hand and on the left? Noble and beneficent in its true outlines, it too may share, may even now be sharing, the liability of the loftiest conceptions to degenerate into catchwords, or into cant. "Liberty, what crimes have been wrought in thy name!" and [220] does not religion share the same reproach, and conscience also? Yet will we not away with any of the three.

The conviction of a nation is the conviction of the mass of the individuals thereof, and each individual has therefore a personal responsibility for the opinion he holds on a question of great national, or international, moment. Let us look, each of us,—and especially each of us who fears God,—into his own inner heart, and ask himself how far, in his personal life, he is prepared to accept arbitration. Is it not so that the reply must be, "In doubtful questions of moment, wherever I possibly can, knowing my necessary, inevitable proneness to one-sided views, I will seek an impartial adviser, that my bias may be corrected; but when that has been done, when I have sought what aid I can, if conscience still commands, it I must obey. From that duty, burdensome though it may be, no man can relieve me. Conscience, diligently consulted, is to the man the voice of God; between God and the man no other arbiter comes." And if this be so, a pledge beforehand is impossible. I cannot bind myself for a future of which I as yet know nothing, to [221] abide by the decision of any other judge than my own conscience. Much humor—less wit—has been expended upon the Emperor of Germany's supposed carefulness to reject arbitration because an infringement of his divine rights; a phrase which may well be no more than a blunt expression of the sense that no third party can relieve a man from the obligations of the position to which he is called by God, and that for the duties of that position the man can confidently expect divine guidance and help. Be that as it may, the divine right of conscience will, among Americans, receive rare challenge.

It has been urged, however, that a higher organization of the nations, the provision of a supreme tribunal issuing and enforcing judgments, settling thereby quarrels and disputed rights, would produce for the nations of the earth a condition analogous to that of the individual citizen of the state, who no longer defends his own cause, nor is bound in conscience to maintain his own sense of right, when the law decides against him. The conception is not novel, not even modern; something much like it was put forth centuries ago [222] by the Papacy concerning its own functions. It contains two fallacies. First, the submission of the individual citizen is to force, to the constitution of which he personally contributes little, save his individual and general assent. To an unjust law he submits under protest, doubtless often silent; but he submits, not because he consents to the wrong, whether to himself personally or to others, but because he cannot help it. This will perhaps be denied, with the assertion that willing, intelligent submission to law, even when unjust, is yielded by most for the general good. One has, however, only to consider the disposition of the average man to evade payment of taxes, to recognize how far force daily enters into the maintenance and execution of law. Nations, on the contrary, since no force exists, or without their volition can exist, to compel them to accept the institution of an authority superior to their own conscience, yield a willing acquiescence to wrong, when they so yield in obedience to an external authority imposed by themselves. The matter is not helped by the fact of a previous promise to accept such decisions. The wrong-doing of an individual, [223] in consequence of an antecedent promise, does not relieve the conscience thus rashly fettered. The ancient warning still stands, "Suffer not thy mouth to cause thy flesh to sin." For the individual or the nation, arbitration is not possible where the decision may violate conscience; it therefore can be accepted only when it is known that interest merely, not duty, will be affected by the judgment, and such knowledge cannot exist antecedent to the difficulty arising.

There is a further—a second—fallacy in the supposed analogy between the submission of individuals to law, and the advocated submission of states to a central tribunal. The law of the state, overwhelming as is its power relatively to that of the individual citizen, can neither bind nor loose in matters pertaining to the conscience. Still less can any tribunal, however solemnly constituted, liberate a state from its obligation to do right; still less, I say, because the state retains, what the individual has in great part lost, the power to maintain what it believes to be right. Many considerations may make it more right—I do not say *more expedient*—for a man or for a nation, to [224] submit to, or to acquiesce in, wrong than to resist; but in such cases it is conscience still that decides where the balance of justice turns distinctly to the side of wrong. It is, I presume, universally admitted, that occasions may arise where conscience not only justifies, but compels, resistance to law; whether it be the Christian citizen refusing to sacrifice, or the free citizen to subject himself to unconstitutional taxation, or to become the instrument of returning the slave to his master. So also for the Christian state. Existing wrong may have to be allowed, lest a greater wrong be done. Conscience only can decide; and for that very reason conscience must be kept free, that it may decide according to its sense of right, when the case is presented.

There is, therefore, the very serious consideration attendant upon what is loosely styled "compulsory" arbitration,—arbitration stipulated, that is, in advance of a question originating, or of its conditions being appreciated,—that a state may thereby do that which a citizen as towards the state does not do; namely, may voluntarily assume a moral obligation to do, or to allow, wrong. And it must be [225] remembered, also, that many of the difficulties which arise among states involve considerations distinctly beyond and higher than law as international law now exists; whereas the advocated Permanent Tribunal, to which the ultra-organizers look, to take cognizance of all cases, must perforce be governed by law as it exists. It is not, in fact, to be supposed that nations will submit themselves to a tribunal, the general principles of which have not been crystallized into a code of some sort.

A concrete instance, however, is always more comprehensible and instructive than a general discussion. Let us therefore take the incidents and conditions which preceded our recent war with Spain. The facts, as seen by us, may, I apprehend, be fairly stated as follows: In the island of Cuba, a powerful military force,—government it scarcely could be called,—foreign to the island, was holding a small portion of it in enforced subjection, and was endeavoring, unsuccessfully, to reduce the remainder. In pursuance of this attempt, measures were adopted that inflicted immense misery and death upon great numbers of the population. Such suffering is indeed attendant upon war; [226] but it may be stated as a fundamental principle of civilized warfare that useless suffering is condemned, and it had become apparent to military eyes that Spain could not subdue the island, nor restore orderly conditions. The suffering was terrible, and was unavailing.

Under such circumstances, does any moral obligation lie upon a powerful neighboring state? Or, more exactly, if there is borne in upon the moral consciousness of a mighty people that such an afflicted community as that of Cuba at their doors is like Lazarus at the gate of the rich man, and that the duty of stopping the evil rests upon them, what is to be done with such a case of conscience? Could the decision of another, whether nation or court, excuse our nation from the ultimate responsibility of its own decision? But, granting that it might have proved expedient to call in other judges, when we had full knowledge of the circumstances, what would have been our dilemma if, conscience commanding one course, we had found ourselves antecedently bound to abide by the conclusions of another arbiter? For let us not deceive ourselves. Absolutely justifiable, nay, imperative, as most of us believe [227] our action to have been, when tried at the bar of conscience, no arbitral court, acceptable to the two nations, would have decided as our own conscience did. A European diplomatist of distinguished reputation, of a small nation likeliest to be unbiassed, so said to me personally, and it is known that more than one of our own ablest international lawyers held that we were acting in defiance of international law as it now exists; just as the men who resisted the Fugitive Slave Law acted in defiance of the statute law of the land. Decision must have gone against us, so these men think, on the legal merits of the case. Of the moral question the arbiter could take no account; it is not there, indeed, that moral questions must find their solution, but in the court of conscience. Referred to arbitration, doubtless the Spanish flag would still fly over Cuba.

There is unquestionably a higher law than Law, concerning obedience to which no other than the man himself, or the state, can give account to Him that shall judge. The freedom of the conscience may be fettered or signed away by him who owes to it allegiance, yet its supremacy, though thus disavowed, cannot be [228] overthrown. The Conference at The Hague has facilitated future recourse to arbitration, by providing means through which, a case arising, a court is more easily constituted, and rules governing its procedure are ready to hand; but it has refrained from any engagements binding states to have recourse to the tribunal thus created. The responsibility of the state to its own conscience remains unimpeached and independent. The progress thus made and thus limited is to a halting place, at which, whether well chosen or not, the nations must perforce stop for a time; and it will be wise to employ that time in considering the bearings, alike of that which has been done, and of that which has been left undone.

Our own country has a special need thus carefully to consider the possible consequences of arbitration, understood in the sense of an antecedent pledge to resort to it; unless under limitations very carefully hedged. There is an undoubted popular tendency in direction of such arbitration, which would be "compulsory" in the highest moral sense,—the compulsion of a promise. The world at large, and we especially, stand at the opening of a new [229] era, concerning whose problems little can be foreseen. Among the peoples, there is manifested intense interest in the maturing of our national convictions, as being, through Asia, new-comers into active international life, concerning whose course it is impossible to predict; and in many quarters, probably in all except Great Britain, the attitude toward us is watchful rather than sympathetic. The experience of Crete and of Armenia does not suggest beneficent results from the arbitration of many counsellors; especially if contrasted with the more favorable issue when Russia, in 1877, acting on her own single initiative, forced by the conscience of her people, herself alone struck the fetters from Bulgaria; or when we ourselves last year, rejecting intermediation, loosed the bonds from Cuba, and lifted the yoke from the neck of the oppressed.

It was inevitable that thoughts like these should recur frequently to one of the writer's habit of thought, when in constant touch with the atmosphere that hung around the Conference, although the latter was by it but little affected. The poet's words, "The Parliament [230] of man, the federation of the world," were much in men's mouths this past summer. There is no denying the beauty of the ideal, but there was apparent also a disposition, in contemplating it, to contemn the slow processes of evolution by which Nature commonly attains her ends, and to impose at once, by convention, the methods that commended themselves to the sanguine. Fruit is not best ripened by premature plucking, nor can the goal be reached by such short cuts. Step by step, in the past, man has ascended by means of the sword, and his more recent gains, as well as present conditions, show that the time has not yet come to kick down the ladder which has so far served him. Three hundred years ago, the people of the land in which the Conference was assembled wrenched with the sword civil and religious peace and national independence from the tyranny of Spain. Then began the disintegration of her empire, and the deliverance of peoples from her oppression, but this was completed only last year, and then again by the sword—of the United States.

In the centuries which have since intervened, what has not "justice, with valor [231] armed," when confronted by evil in high places, found itself compelled to effect by resort to the sword? To it was due the birth of our own nation, not least among the benefits of which was the stern experience that has made Great Britain no longer the mistress, but the mother, of her dependencies. The control, to good from evil, of the devastating fire of the French Revolution and of Napoleon was due to the sword. The long line of illustrious names and deeds, of those who bore it not in vain, has in our times culminated—if indeed the end is even yet nearly reached—in the new birth of the United States by the extirpation of human slavery, and in the downfall, but yesterday, of a colonial empire identified with tyranny. What the sword, and it supremely, tempered only by the stern demands of justice and of conscience, and the loving voice of charity, has done for India and for Egypt, is a tale at once too long and too well known for repetition here. Peace, indeed, is not adequate to all progress; there are resistances that can be overcome only by explosion. What means less violent than war would in a half-year have [232] solved the Caribbean problem, shattered national ideas deep rooted in the prepossessions of a century, and planted the United States in Asia, face to face with the great world problem of the immediate future? What but war rent the veil which prevented the English-speaking communities from seeing eye to eye, and revealed to each the face of a brother? Little wonder that a war which, with comparatively little bloodshed, brought such consequences, was followed by the call for a Peace Conference!

Power, force, is a faculty of national life; one of the talents committed to nations by God. Like every other endowment of a complex organization, it must be held under control of the enlightened intellect and of the upright heart; but no more than any other can it be carelessly or lightly abjured, without incurring the responsibility of one who buries in the earth that which was intrusted to him for use. And this obligation to maintain right, by force if need be, while common to all states, rests peculiarly upon the greater, in proportion to their means. Much is required of those to whom much is given. So viewed, the ability speedily to put forth the nation's power, by [233] adequate organization and other necessary preparation, according to the reasonable demands of the nation's intrinsic strength and of its position in the world, is one of the clear duties involved in the Christian word "watchfulness,"—readiness for the call that may come, whether expectedly or not. Until it is demonstrable that no evil exists, or threatens the world, which cannot be obviated without recourse to force, the obligation to readiness must remain; and, where evil is mighty and defiant, the obligation to use force—that is, war—arises. Nor is it possible, antecedently, to bring these conditions and obligations under the letter of precise and codified law, to be administered by a tribunal; and in the spirit legalism is marked by blemishes as real as those commonly attributed to "militarism," and not more elevated. The considerations which determine good and evil, right and wrong, in crises of national life, or of the world's history, are questions of equity often too complicated for decision upon mere rules, or even principles, of law, international or other. The instances of Bulgaria, of Armenia, and of Cuba, are entirely in point, and it is most probable that [234] the contentions about the future of China will afford further illustration. Even in matters where the interest of nations is concerned, the moral element enters; because each generation in its day is the guardian of those which shall follow it. Like all guardians, therefore, while it has the power to act according to its best judgment, it has no right, for the mere sake of peace, to permit known injustice to be done to its wards.

The present strong feeling, throughout the nations of the world, in favor of arbitration, is in itself a subject for congratulation almost unalloyed. It carries indeed a promise, to the certainty of which no paper covenants can pretend; for it influences the conscience by inward conviction, not by external fetter. But it must be remembered that such sentiments, from their very universality and evident laudableness, need correctives, for they bear in themselves a great danger of excess or of precipitancy. Excess is seen in the disposition, far too prevalent, to look upon war not only as an evil, but as an evil unmixed, unnecessary, and therefore always unjustifiable; while precipitancy, to reach results considered desirable, is [235] evidenced by the wish to *impose* arbitration, to prevent recourse to war, by a general pledge previously made. Both frames of mind receive expression in the words of speakers, among whom a leading characteristic is lack of measuredness and of proportion. Thus an eminent citizen is reported to have said: "There is no more occasion for two nations to go to war than for two men to settle their difficulties with clubs." Singularly enough, this point of view assumes to represent peculiarly Christian teaching, willingly ignorant of the truth that Christianity, while it will not force the conscience by other than spiritual weapons, as "compulsory" arbitration might, distinctly recognizes the sword as the resister and remedier of evil in the sphere "of this world."

Arbitration's great opportunity has come in the advancing moral standards of states, whereby the disposition to deliberate wrong-doing has diminished, and consequently the occasions for redressing wrong by force the less frequent to arise. In view of recent events however, and very especially of notorious, high-handed oppression, initiated since the calling of the Peace Conference, and resolutely [236] continued during its sessions in defiance of the public opinion—the conviction—of the world at large, it is premature to assume that such occasions belong wholly to the past. Much less can it be assumed that there will be no further instances of a community believing, conscientiously and entirely, that honor and duty require of it a certain course, which another community with equal integrity may hold to be inconsistent with the rights and obligations of its own members. It is quite possible, especially to one who has recently visited Holland, to conceive that Great Britain and the Boers are alike satisfied of the substantial justice of their respective claims. It is permissible most earnestly to hope that, in disputes between sovereign states, arbitration may find a way to reconcile peace with fidelity to conscience, in the case of both; but if the conviction of conscience remains unshaken, war is better than disobedience,—better than acquiescence in recognized wrong. The great danger of undiscriminating advocacy of arbitration, which threatens even the cause it seeks to maintain, is that it may lead men to tamper with equity, to compromise with [237] unrighteousness, soothing their conscience with the belief that war is so entirely wrong that beside it no other tolerated evil is wrong. Witness Armenia, and witness Crete. War has been avoided; but what of the national consciences that beheld such iniquity and withheld the hand?

Note.—This paper was the means of bringing into the author's hands a letter by the late General Sherman, which forcibly illustrates how easily, in quiet moments, men forget what they have owed, and still owe, to the sword. From the coincidence of its thought with that of the article itself, permission to print it here has been asked and received.

New York , February 5th, 1890.

Dear General Meigs ,—I attended the Centennial Ceremonies in honor of the Supreme Court yesterday, four full hours in the morning at the Metropolitan Opera House, and about the same measure of time at the Grand Banquet of 850 lawyers in the evening at the Lenox Lyceum.

The whole was superb in all its proportions, but it was no place for a soldier. I was bidden to the feast solely and exclusively because in 1858 for a few short months I was an attorney at Leavenworth, Kansas.

The Bar Association of the United States has manifestly cast aside the Sword of Liberty. Justice and Law have ignored the significance of the Great Seal of the United States, with its emblematic olive branch and thirteen arrows, "all proper," and now claim that, without force, Law and moral suasion have carried us through one hundred years of history. Of course, in your study you will read at leisure these speeches, and if in them you discover any sense of obligation to the Soldier element, you will be luckier than I, a listener.

[238] From 1861 to 1865 the Supreme Court was absolutely paralyzed; their decrees and writs were treated with contempt south of the Potomac and Ohio; they could not summon a witness or send a Deputy Marshal. War, and the armed Power of the Nation, alone removed the barrier and restored to the U.S. courts their lawful jurisdiction. Yet, from these honied words of flattery, a stranger would have inferred that at last the lawyers of America had discovered the sovereign panacea of a Government without force, either visible or in reserve.

I was in hopes the Civil War had dispelled this dangerous illusion, but it seems not.

You and I can fold our hands and truly say we have done a man's share, and leave the consequences to younger men who must buffet with the next storms; but a Government which ignores the great truths illuminated in heraldic language over its very Capitol is not yet at the end of its woes.

With profound respect,
W.T. Sherman .

[239]

THE RELATIONS OF THE UNITED STATES TO THEIR NEW DEPENDENCIES

[240]
[241]

THE RELATIONS OF THE UNITED STATES TO THEIR NEW DEPENDENCIES
ToC

In modern times there have been two principal colonizing nations, which not merely have occupied and administered a great transmarine domain, but have impressed upon it their own identity—the totality of their political and racial characteristics—to a degree that is likely to affect permanently the history of the world at large.

These two nations, it is needless to say, are Great Britain and Spain. Russia, their one competitor, differs from them in that her sustained advance over alien regions is as wholly by land as theirs has been by sea. France and Holland have occupied and administered, and continue to occupy and administer, large extents of territory; but it is scarcely necessary to argue that in neither case has the race possessed the land, nor have the national characteristics been transmitted to the dwellers [242] therein as a whole. They have realized, rather, the idea recently formulated by Mr. Benjamin Kidd for the development of tropical regions,—administration from without.

The unexpected appearance of the United States as in legal control of transmarine territory, which as yet they have not had opportunity either to occupy or to administer, coincides in time with the final downfall of Spain's colonial empire, and with a stage in the upward progress of that of Great Britain, so marked, in the contrast it presents to the ruin of Spain, as to compel attention and comparison, with an ultimate purpose to draw therefrom instruction for the United States in the new career forced upon them. The larger colonies of Great Britain are not indeed reaching their majority, for that they did long ago; but the idea formulated in the phrase "imperial federation" shows that they, and the mother country herself, have passed through and left behind the epoch when the accepted thought in both was that they should in the end separate, as sons leave the father's roof, to set up, each for himself. To that transition phase has succeeded the ideal of partnership, [243] more complex indeed and difficult of attainment, but trebly strong if realized. The terms of partnership, the share of each member in the burdens and in the profits, present difficulties which will delay, and may prevent, the consummation; time alone can show. The noticeable factor in this change of mind, however, is the affectionate desire manifested by both parent and children to ensure the desired end. Between nations long alien we have high warrant for saying that interest alone determines action; but between communities of the same blood, and when the ties of dependence on the one part are still recent, sentiments—love and mutual pride—are powerful, provided there be good cause for them. And good cause there is. Since she lost what is now the United States, Great Britain has become benevolent and beneficent to her colonies.

It is not in colonies only, however, that Great Britain has been beneficent to weaker communities; nor are benevolence and beneficence the only qualities she has shown. She has been strong also,—strong in her own interior life, whence all true strength issues; strong in the quality of the men she has sent forth to [244] colonize and to administer; strong to protect by the arm of her power, by land, and, above all, by sea. The advantage of the latter safeguard is common to all her dependencies; but it is among subject and alien races, and not in colonies properly so called, that her terrestrial energy chiefly manifests itself, to control, to protect, and to elevate. Of these functions, admirably discharged in the main, India and Egypt are the conspicuous illustrations. In them she administers from without, and cannot be said to colonize, for the land was already full.

Conspicuous result constitutes example: for imitation, if honorable; for warning, if shameful. Experience is the great teacher, and is at its best when personal; but in the opening of a career such experience is wanting to the individual, and must be sought in the record of other lives, or of other nations. The United States are just about to enter on a task of government—of administration—over regions which, in inhabitants, in climate, and in political tradition, differ essentially from themselves. What are the conditions of success?

We have the two great examples. Great Britain has been, in the main, and increasingly, [245] beneficent and strong. Spain, from the very first, as the records show, was inhumanly oppressive to the inferior races; and, after her own descendants in the colonies became aliens in habit to the home country, she to them also became tyrannically exacting. But, still more, Spain became weaker and weaker as the years passed, the tyranny of her extortions being partially due to exigencies of her political weakness and to her economical declension. Let us, however, not fail to observe that the beneficence, as well as the strength, of Great Britain has been a matter of growth. She was not always what she now is to the alien subject. There is, therefore, no reason to despair, as some do, that the United States, who share her traditions, can attain her success. The task is novel to us; we may make blunders; but, guided by her experience, we should reach the goal more quickly.

And it is to our interest to do so. Enlightened self-interest demands of us to recognize not merely, and in general, the imminence of the great question of the farther East, which is rising so rapidly before us, but also, specifically, the importance to us of a strong and beneficent [246] occupation of adjacent territory. In the domain of color, black and white are contradictory; but it is not so with self-interest and beneficence in the realm of ideas. This paradox is now too generally accepted for insistence, although in the practical life of states the proper order of the two is too often inverted. But, where the relations are those of trustee to ward, as are those of any state which rules over a weaker community not admitted to the full privileges of home citizenship, the first test to which measures must be brought is the good of the ward. It is the first interest of the guardian, for it concerns his honor. Whatever the part of the United States in the growing conflict of European interests around China and the East, we deal there with equals, and may battle like men; but our new possessions, with their yet minor races, are the objects only of solicitude.

Ideas underlie action. If the paramount idea of beneficence becomes a national conviction, we may stumble and err, we may at times sin, or be betrayed by unworthy representatives; but we shall advance unfailingly. I have been asked to contribute to the discussion of this matter something from my own usual point of [247] view; which is, of course, the bearing of sea power upon the security and the progress of nations. Well, one great element of sea power, which, it will be remembered, is commercial before it is military, is that there be territorial bases of action in the regions important to its commerce. That is self-interest. But the history of Spain's decline, and the history of Great Britain's advance,—in the latter of which the stern lesson given by the revolt of the United States is certainly a conspicuous factor, as also, perhaps, the other revolt known as the Indian Mutiny, in 1857,—alike teach us that territories beyond the sea can be securely held only when the advantage and interests of the inhabitants are the primary object of the administration. The inhabitants may not return love for their benefits,—comprehension or gratitude may fail them; but the sense of duty achieved, and the security of the tenure, are the reward of the ruler.

I have understood also that, through the pages of "The Engineering Magazine," I should speak to the men who stand at the head of the great mechanical industries of the country,—the great inventors and the leaders in home [248] development,—and that they would be willing to hear me. But what can I say to them that they do not know? Their own businesses are beyond my scope and comprehension. The opportunities offered by the new acquisitions of the United States to the pursuits with which they are identified they can understand better than I. Neither is it necessary to say that adequate—nay, great—naval development is a condition of success, although such an assertion is more within my competence, as a student of navies and of history. That form of national strength which is called sea power becomes now doubly incumbent. It is needed not merely for national self-assertion, but for beneficence; to ensure to the new subjects of the nation peace and industry, uninterrupted by wars, the great protection against which is preparation—to use that one counsel of Washington's which the anti-imperialist considers to be out of date.

I have, therefore, but one thing which I have not already often said to offer to such men, who affect these great issues through their own aptitudes and through their far-reaching influence upon public opinion, which they touch [249] through many channels. Sea power, as a national interest, commercial and military, rests not upon fleets only, but also upon local territorial bases in distant commercial regions. It rests upon them most securely when they are extensive, and when they have a numerous population bound to the sovereign country by those ties of interest which rest upon the beneficence of the ruler; of which beneficence power to protect is not the least factor. Mere just dealing and protection, however, do not exhaust the demands of beneficence towards alien subjects, still in race-childhood. The firm but judicious remedying of evils, the opportunities for fuller and happier lives, which local industries and local development afford, these also are a part of the duty of the sovereign power. Above all, there must be constant recognition that self-interest and beneficence alike demand that the local welfare be first taken into account. It is possible, of course, that it may at times have to yield to the necessities of the whole body; but it should be first considered.

The task is great; who is sufficient for it? The writer believes firmly in the ultimate power of ideas. Napoleon is reported to have said: [250] "Imagination rules the world." If this be generally so, how much more the true imaginations which are worthy to be called ideas! There is a nobility in man which welcomes the appeal to beneficence. May it find its way quickly now to the heads and hearts of the American people, before less worthy ambitions fill them; and, above all, to the kings of men, in thought and in action, under whose leadership our land makes its giant strides. There is in this no Quixotism. Materially, the interest of the nation is one with its beneficence; but if the ideas get inverted, and the nation sees in its new responsibilities, first of all, markets and profits, with incidental resultant benefit to the natives, it will go wrong. Through such mistakes Great Britain passed. She lost the United States; she suffered bitter anguish in India; but India and Egypt testify to-day to the nobility of her repentance. Spain repented not. The examples are before us. Which shall we follow?

And is there not a stimulus to our imagination, and to high ambition, to read, as we easily may, how the oppressed have been freed, and the degraded lifted, in India and in Egypt, not [251] only by political sagacity and courage, but by administrative capacity directing the great engineering enterprises, which change the face of a land and increase a hundredfold the opportunities for life and happiness? The profession of the writer, and the subject consequently of most of his writing, stands for organized force, which, if duly developed, is the concrete expression of the nation's strength. But while he has never concealed his opinion that the endurance of civilization, during a future far beyond our present foresight, depends ultimately upon due organization of force, he has ever held, and striven to say, that such force is but the means to an end, which end is durable peace and progress, and therefore beneficence. The triumphs and the sufferings of the past months have drawn men's eyes to the necessity for increase of force, not merely to sustain over-sea dominion, but also to ensure timely use, in action, of the latent military and naval strength which the nation possesses. The speedy and inevitable submission of Spain has demonstrated beyond contradiction the primacy of navies in determining the issue of transmarine wars; for after Cavité and [252] Santiago had crippled hopelessly the enemy's navy, the end could not be averted, though it might have been postponed. On the other hand, the numerical inadequacy of the troops sent to Santiago, and their apparently inadequate equipment, have shown the necessity for greater and more skilfully organized land forces. The deficiency of the United States in this respect would have permitted a prolonged resistance by the enemy's army in Cuba,—a course which, though sure ultimately to fail, appealed strongly to military punctilio.

These lessons are so obvious that it is not supposable that the national intelligence, which has determined the American demand for the Philippines, can overlook them; certainly not readers of the character of those to whom this paper is primarily addressed. But when all this has been admitted and provided for, it still remains that force is but the minister, under whose guardianship industry does its work and enjoys peaceably the fruits of its labor. To the mechanical industries of the country, in their multifold forms, our new responsibilities propound the questions, not [253] merely of naval and military protection, but of material development, which, first beneficent to the inhabitants and to the land, gives also, and thereby, those firm foundations of a numerous and contented population, and of ample local resources, upon which alone military power can securely rest.

[254]
[255]

DISTINGUISHING QUALITIES OF
SHIPS OF WAR

[256]
[257]

DISTINGUISHING QUALITIES OF
SHIPS OF WAR ToC

From the descriptions of warships usually published, it would naturally be inferred that the determination of their various qualities concern primarily the naval architect and the marine engineer. This is an error. Warships exist for war. Their powers, being for the operations of war, are military necessities, the appreciation of which, and the consequent qualities demanded, are military questions. Only when these have been decided, upon military reasons, begins the office of the technologist; namely, to produce the qualities prescribed by the sea officer. An eminent British naval architect used to say, "I hold that it is the part of the naval officers to tell us just what qualities—speed, gun-power, armor, coal endurance, etc.—are required in a ship to be built, and then leave it to us to produce the ship." These words distinguish accurately and [258] summarily the functions of the military and the technical experts in the development of navies. It is from the military standpoint, solely, that this article is written.

The military function of a navy is to control the sea, so far as the sea contributes to the maintenance of the war. The sea is the theatre of naval war; it is the field in which the naval campaign is waged; and, like other fields of military operations, it does not resemble a blank sheet of paper, every point of which is equally important with every other point. Like the land, the sea, as a military field, has its important centres, and it is not controlled by spreading your force, whatever its composition, evenly over an entire field of operations, like butter over bread, but by occupying the centres with aggregated forces—fleets or armies—ready to act in masses, in various directions from the centres. This commonplace of warfare is its first principle. It is called concentration, because the forces are not spread out, but drawn together at the centres which for the moment are most important.

Concentrated forces, therefore, are those [259] upon which warfare depends for efficient control, and for efficient energy in the operations of war. They have two chief essential characteristics: force, which is gained by concentration of numbers; and mobility, which is the ability to carry the force rapidly, as well as effectively, from the centre to any point of the outlying field where action, offensive or defensive, becomes necessary. It is essential to keep in mind both these factors, and to study them in their true mutual relations of priority, in order and in importance,—force first, mobility second; for the force does not exist for the mobility, but the mobility for the force, which it subserves. Force without mobility is useful; even though limited, as in coast fortifications; mobility without force is almost useless for the greater purposes of war. Consequently, when it is found, as is frequently the case, that one must yield somewhat, in order to the full development of the other, it is extreme mobility, extreme speed, which must give way to greater force.

This caution may seem superfluous, but it is not so; for in the popular fancy, and in the appreciation of the technical expert, and to [260] some extent also in the official mind as well,—owing to that peculiar fad of the day which lays all stress on machinery,—mobility, speed, is considered the most important characteristic in every kind of ship of war. Let the reader ask himself what is the most pronounced impression left upon his mind by newspaper accounts of a new ship. Is it not that she is expected to make so many knots? Compared with that, what does the average man know of the fighting she can do, when she has reached the end of that preposterously misleading performance called her trial trip? The error is of the nature of a half-truth, the most dangerous of errors; for it is true that, as compared with land forces, the great characteristic of navies is mobility; but it is not true that, between different classes of naval vessels, the swiftest are the most efficient for control of the sea. Force is for that the determining element.

Keeping these relations of force and mobility constantly in mind, there is a further consideration, easily evident, but which needs to be distinctly stated and remembered. When a ship is once built, she cannot be divided. If [261] you have on land concentrated ten thousand men, you can detach any fraction of them you wish for a particular purpose; you can send one man or ten, or a company, or a regiment. You can, in short, make of them any fresh combination you choose. With ships, the least you can send is one ship, and the smallest you have may be more than you wish to spare. From this (as well as for other reasons) arises a necessity for ships of different classes and sizes, which must be determined beforehand. The determination must be reached not merely by *a priori* reasoning, as though the problem were wholly new; but regard must be had to the experience of the past,—to the teaching of history. History is experience, and as such underlies progress, just as the cognate idea, experiment, underlies scientific advance.

Both history and reasoning, of the character already outlined in these papers, concur in telling us that control of the sea is exercised by vessels individually very large for their day, concentrated into bodies called fleets, stationed at such central points as the emergency demands. Our predecessors of the past two centuries called these vessels "ships of the line [262] of battle," from which probably derives our briefer modern name "battleship," which is appropriate only if the word "battle" be confined to fleet actions.

Among the naval entities, fleets are at once the most powerful and the least mobile; yet they are the only really determining elements in naval war. They are the most powerful, because in them are concentrated many ships, each of which is extremely strong for fighting. They are the least mobile, because many ships, which must keep together, can proceed only at the rate of the slowest among them. It is natural to ask why not build them all equally fast? The reply is, it is possible to do so within very narrow limits, but it is not possible to keep them so. Every deterioration, accident, or adverse incident, which affects one involves all, as regards speed, though not as regards fighting force. In our recent war, when an extensive operation was contemplated, the speed of one battleship reduced the calculated speed of the fleet by one knot,—one sea mile per hour. But, it may be urged, will not your slowest speed be much increased, if every vessel be originally faster? Doubtless; but speed means [263] tonnage,—part of the ship's weight devoted to engines; and weight, if given to speed, is taken from other qualities; and if, to increase speed, you reduce fighting power, you increase something you cannot certainly hold, at the expense of something at once much more important and more constant—less liable to impairment. In the operation just cited the loss of speed was comparatively of little account; but the question of fighting force upon arrival was serious.

An escape from this dilemma is sought by the advocates of very high speed for battleships by increasing the size of the individual ship. If this increase of size is accompanied by increase of speed, but not proportionately of fighting power, the measure, in the opinion of the writer, stands self-condemned. But, granting that force gains equally with speed, there is a further objection already mentioned. The exigencies of war demand at times division, as well as concentration; and, in fact, concentration, properly understood, does not mean keeping ships necessarily within sight of one another, but so disposed that they can unite readily at will,—a consideration which space forbids me more than to state. Now, a big ship [264] cannot be divided into two; or, more pertinently, eight ships cannot be made into ten when you want two bodies of five each. The necessity, or supposed necessity, of maintaining the Flying Squadron at Hampton Roads during the late hostilities exactly illustrates this idea. Under all the conditions, this disposition was not wholly false to concentration, rightly considered; but had the ships been fewer and bigger, it could not have been made.

The net result, therefore, of the argument, supported, as the writer believes, by the testimony of history, is: (1) that a navy which wishes to affect decisively the issues of a maritime war must be composed of heavy ships—"battleships"—possessing a maximum of fighting power, and so similar in type as to facilitate that uniformity of movement and of evolution upon which concentration, once effected, must depend for its maintenance, whether during a passage or in actual engagement; (2) that in such ships, regarded as fighting factors, which is their primary function, size is limited, as to the minimum, by the advisability of concentrating as much fighting power as possible under the hand of a single captain; but, on the other [265] hand, size is also limited, as to its maximum, by the need of retaining ability to subdivide the whole fleet, according to particular exigencies; (3) as regards that particular form of mobility called speed, the writer regards it as distinctly secondary for the battleship; that, to say the least, the present proportions of weight assigned to fighting force should not be sacrificed to obtain increase of speed. Neither should the size of the individual ships be increased merely to obtain rates of speed higher than that already shown by some of our present battleships.

Concerning that particular function of mobility which is called coal endurance,—that is, the ability to steam a certain distance without stopping to recoal,—the convenience to military operations of such a quality is evident; but it is obvious that it cannot, with the fuels now available, be possessed beyond very narrow limits. A battleship that can steam the greatest distance that separates two fortified coaling stations of her nation, with a reasonable margin above that to meet emergencies, will evidently be able to remain for a long while with the fleet, when this is concentrated to remain under [266] reduced steam at a particular point. The recoaling of ships is a difficulty which must be met by improving the methods of that operation, not by sacrificing the military considerations which should control the size and other qualities of the vessel.

It is the belief of the writer that ten thousand tons represent very nearly the minimum, and twelve thousand the maximum, of size for the battleship. Our present battleships fall within those limits, and, although less uniform in their qualities than might be desired, they give perfectly satisfactory indications that the requisite qualities can all be had without increase of size. When more is wanted—and we should always be striving for perfection—it should be sought in the improvement of processes, and not in the adding of ton to ton, like a man running up a bill. It is the difference between economy and extravagance. Into battleships such as these should go the greater proportion of the tonnage a nation gives to its navy. Ships so designed may reach the ground of action later than those which have more speed; but when they arrive, the enemy, if of weaker fighting power, must go, and what [267] then has been the good of their speed? War is won by holding on, or driving off; not by successful running away.

An important consideration in determining the necessary composition of a navy is the subdivision of fighting power into offensive and defensive. The latter is represented chiefly by armor, the former by guns; although other factors contribute to both. The relative importance of the two depends upon no mere opinion of the writer, but upon a consensus of authority practically unanimous, and which, therefore, demands no argument, but simple statement. Offensive action—not defensive—determines the issues of war. "The best defence against the enemy's fire is a rapid fire from our own guns," was a pithy phrase of our Admiral Farragut; and in no mere punning sense it may be added that it is for this reason that the rapid-fire gun of the present day made such big strides in professional favor, the instant it was brought to the test of battle. The rapid-fire gun is smaller than the great cannon mounted in the turrets; but, while the latter have their proper usefulness, the immensely larger number of projectiles fired in a given [268] time, and valid against the target presented to them, makes the rapid-fire battery a much stronger weapon, offensively, than the slow-acting giants. Here is the great defect of the monitor, properly so-called; that is, the low-freeboard monitor. Defensively, the monitor is very strong; offensively, judged by present-day standards, it is weak, possessing the heavy cannon, but deficient in rapid fire. Consequently, its usefulness is limited chiefly to work against fortifications,—a target exceptional in resistance, and rarely a proper object for naval attack. It is the opinion of the writer that no more monitors should be built, except as accessory to the defence of those harbors where submarine mines cannot be depended upon,—as at San Francisco and Puget Sound. It should be added that the monitor at sea rolls twice as rapidly as the battleship, which injuriously affects accuracy of aim; that is, offensive power.

The general principle of the decisive superiority of offensive power over defensive is applicable throughout,—to the operations of a war, to the design of a battleship, to the scheme of building a whole navy. It is to the erroneous belief in mere defence that we [269] owe much of the faith in the monitor, and some of the insistence upon armor; while the cry that went up for local naval defence along our coast, when war threatened in the spring of 1898, showed an ignorance of the first principles of warfare, which, if not resisted, would have left us impotent even before Spain.

Brief mention only can be given to the other classes of vessels needed by the navy. Concerning them, one general remark must be made. They are subsidiary to the fighting fleet, and represent rather that subdivision of a whole navy which is opposed to the idea of concentration, upon which the battleship rests. As already noted, a built ship cannot be divided; therefore, battleships must be supplemented by weaker or smaller vessels, to perform numerous detached and often petty services.

From this characteristic of detachment—often singly—important engagements will rarely be fought by these smaller vessels. Therefore, in them fighting power declines in relative importance, and speed, to perform their missions, increases in proportion. As their essential use is not to remain at the centres, but to move about, they are called [270] generically cruisers, from the French word *croiser*,—to cross. They cross back and forth, they rove the sea,—despatch boats, lookouts, scouts, or raiders. They are the cavalry of the fleet.

Prominent among these in modern navies is the so-called "armored" cruiser,—a type to which belonged the four principal vessels of Cervera's squadron. The name itself is interesting, as indicating the inveterate tendency of mankind to straddle,—the reluctance to choose one of two opposite things, and frankly to give up the other. Armor, being an element of fighting power, belongs properly to the battleship rather than the cruiser; and in the latter, if the weight spent in armor detracts from speed or coal endurance, it contravenes the leading idea of a cruiser,—mobility. But, while the name is incongruous, the type has its place as an armored vessel, though not as a cruiser. In our service at least—where it is represented by the *New York* and the *Brooklyn*—it is practically a second-class battleship, in which weight taken from fighting power is given to enginery and to speed. The advantage arising from this is purely [271] tactical; that is, it comes into play only when in touch with the enemy. The armored cruiser belongs with the fleet, therefore her superior speed does not tell in making passages; but when fleets are in presence, or in the relative conditions of chase and pursuit, there is an advantage in being able to throw to the front, rear, or flanks, vessels which on a pinch can either fight or fly. This, be it noted in passing, is no new thing, but as old as naval history. A squadron of fast battleships of the day, thrown to the front of a fleet to harass the flanks of the enemy, is a commonplace of naval tactics, alike of galleys and sailing ships. Off Santiago, the *New York* and *Brooklyn* were, by Admiral Sampson, placed on the flanks of his squadron. Whichever way Cervera turned he would find a vessel of speed and fighting power equal to those of his own ships. Though unequal in fighting power to a first-class battleship, many circumstances may arise which would justify the armored cruiser in engaging one, provided her own fleet was in supporting distance. From their hybrid type, and from the exceptional circumstances under which they can be used, the [272] tonnage put into these vessels should be but a small percentage of that given to the battle fleet, to which, and not to the cruisers, they really belong.

Concerning all other cruisers, mobility, represented in speed and coal endurance, is the chief requisite. Notwithstanding occasional aberrations in the past, the development of the cruiser classes may be safely entrusted by the public to the technical experts; provided it be left to naval officers, military men, to say what qualities should predominate. Moreover, as such vessels generally act singly, it is of less importance that they vary much in type, and the need of subdivision carries with it that of numerous sizes; but battleships, including armored cruisers, are meant to work together, and insistence should be made upon homogeneousness, especially in manœuvring qualities.

To sum up: the attention of the public should be centred upon the armored fleet, to which the bulk of expenditure should be devoted; the monitor, pure and simple,—save for very exceptional uses,—should be eliminated; the development of the true cruiser,—not armored,—both in type and in numbers, [273] does not require great interest of the public; much of the duties of this class, also, can be discharged fairly well by purchased vessels, although such will never have the proportion of fighting power which every type of ship of war should possess. As a rule, it is undesirable that a military force, land or sea, should have to retreat before one of equal size, as auxiliary cruisers often would.

[274]
[275]

CURRENT FALLACIES UPON NAVAL SUBJECTS

[276]
[277]

CURRENT FALLACIES UPON NAVAL SUBJECTS ToC

All matters connected with the sea tend to have, in a greater or less degree, a distinctly specialized character, due to the unfamiliarity which the sea, as a scene of *action*, has for the mass of mankind. Nothing is more trite than the remark continually made to naval officers, that life at sea must give them a great deal of leisure for reading and other forms of personal culture. Without going so far as to say that there is no more leisure in a naval officer's life than in some other pursuits—social engagements, for instance, are largely eliminated when at sea—there is very much less than persons imagine; and what there is is broken up by numerous petty duties and incidents, of which people living on shore have no conception, because they have no experience. It is evident that the remark proceeds in most cases from the speaker's own consciousness of [278] the unoccupied monotony of an ocean passage, in which, unless exceptionally observant, he has not even detected the many small but essential functions discharged by the officers of the ship, whom he sees moving about, but the aim of whose movements he does not understand. The passenger, as regards the economy of the vessel, is passive; he fails to comprehend, often even to perceive, the intense functional activity of brain and body which goes on around him—the real life of the organism.

In the progress of the world, nautical matters of every kind are to most men what the transactions of a single ship are to the passenger. They receive impressions, which they mistake for opinions—a most common form of error. These impressions are repeated from mouth to mouth, and having the common note of superficial observation, they are found to possess a certain resemblance. So they serve mutually to fortify one another, and to constitute a *quasi* public opinion. The repetition and stereotyping of impressions are greatly forwarded by the system of organized gossip which we call the press.

It is in consequence of this, quite as much [279] as of the extravagances in a certain far from reputable form of journalism, that the power of the press, great as it unquestionably still is, is not what it should be. It intensifies the feeling of its own constituents, who usually take the paper because they agree with it; but if candid representation of all sides constitutes a fair attempt to instruct the public, no man expects a matter to be fairly put forward. So far does this go, in the experience of the present writer, that one of the most reputable journals in the country, in order to establish a certain extreme position, quoted his opinion in one paragraph, while omitting to give the carefully guarded qualification expressed in the very succeeding paragraph; whereby was conveyed, by implication, the endorsement of the extreme opinion advocated, which the writer certainly never held.

Direct misrepresentation, however, whether by commission or by omission, careless or wilful, is probably less harmful than the indirect injury produced by continual repetition of unintentional misconceptions. The former occurs generally in the case of living, present-moment questions; it reaches chiefly those already [280] convinced; and it has its counteraction in the arguments of the other party, which are read by the appropriate constituency. The real work of those questions of the day goes on behind the scenes; and the press affects them, not because of its intrinsic power, but only in so far as it is thought to represent the trend of thought in a body of voters. On subjects of less immediate moment, as military and naval matters are—except when war looms near, and preparation is too late—men's brains, already full enough of pressing cares, refuse to work, and submit passively to impressions, as the eye, without conscious action, takes note of and records external incidents. Unfortunately these impressions, uncorrected by reflection, exaggerated in narration, and intensified by the repetition of a number of writers, come to constitute a body of public belief, not strictly rational in its birth or subsequent growth, but as impassive in its resistance to argument as it was innocent of mental process during its formation.

The intention of the present paper is to meet, and as far as possible to remove, some such current errors of the day on naval [281] matters—popular misconceptions, continually encountered in conversation and in the newspapers.

Accepting the existence of the navy, and the necessity for its continuance—for some starting-point must be assumed—the errors to be touched upon are:

1. That the United States needs a navy "for defence only."

2. That a navy "for defence only" means for the immediate defence of our seaports and coast-line; an allowance also being made for scattered cruisers to prey upon an enemy's commerce.

3. That if we go beyond this, by acquiring any territory overseas, either by negotiation or conquest, we step at once to the need of having a navy larger than the largest, which is that of Great Britain, now the largest in the world.

4. That the difficulty of doing this,

and the expense involved, are the greater because of the rapid advances in naval improvement, which it is gravely said make a ship obsolete in a very few years; or, to use a very favorite hyperbole, she becomes obsolete before she can be launched. The assertion of the rapid [282] obsolescence of ships of war will be dwelt upon, in the hopes of contravening it.

5. After this paper had been written, the calamity to the United States ship *Maine*, in the harbor of Havana, elicited, from the mourning and consternation of the country, the evident tokens of other unreasoning apprehensions—springing from imperfect knowledge and vague impressions—which at least should be noticed cursorily, and if possible appeased.

First, the view that the United States should plan its navy—in numbers and in sizes of ships—for defence only, rests upon a confusion of ideas—a political idea and a military idea—under the one term of "defence." Politically, it has always been assumed in the United States, and very properly, that our policy should never be wantonly aggressive; that we should never seek our own advantage, however evident, by an unjust pressure upon another nation, much less by open war. This, it will be seen, is a political idea, one which serves for the guidance of the people and of the statesmen of the country in determining—not *how* war is to be carried on, which is a military question, but—under what [283] circumstances war is permissible, or unjust. This is a question of civil policy, pure and simple, and by no means a military question. As a nation, we have always vehemently avowed that we will, and do, act justly; in practice, like other states, and like mankind generally, when we have wanted anything very badly, we have—at least at times—managed to see that it was just that we should have it. In the matter of general policy our hands are by no means clean from aggression. General Grant, after retiring from public life, maintained that the war with Mexico was an unjust war; a stigma which, if true, stains our possession of California and much other territory. The acquisition of Louisiana was as great an outrage upon the technical rights of Spain as the acquisition of Hawaii would be upon the technical rights of the fast-disappearing aborigines; and there can be little doubt that, although we did not go to war with Spain to get Florida, we made things so uncomfortable for her that she was practically forced at last to get out. It does not follow necessarily that any of these actions were wrong, even if we consider that the so-called *legal* rights of Mexico and Spain [284] were set aside by the strong hand; for law is simply an invention of mankind to secure justice, and when justice, the natural rights of the greater number, is prevented by the legal, not the natural, rights of a few, the latter may be set aside, as it is at every election, where large minorities of people are forced to submit to what they consider grievous wrong. The danger incurred by overleaping law to secure what is right may be freely admitted; but no great responsibility, such as the use of power always is, can be exercised at all without some danger of abuse. However, be that as it may, there can be no question that in times past we have aggressed upon the legal rights of other states; and in the annexation of Louisiana we infringed the letter of our own Constitution. We broke the law in order to reach an end eminently beneficial to the majority of those concerned. Nevertheless, while thus aggressive on occasion, warring for offence and not for defence only, it is distinctly a good thing that we hold up the ideal, and persuade ourselves that we cherish it; that we prepare means of war only for defence. It is better honestly to profess a high standard, even if we [285] fall from it at times, than wilfully to adopt a lower ideal of conduct.

The phrase "War for defence only" conveys, therefore, a political idea, and, as such, a proper and noble idea. Unfortunately, in our country, where almost all activities fall under two chief heads—politics and business—politics, the less sensitively organized but more forceful of the two, intrudes everywhere and masters everything. We dread standing armies. Why? Because standing armies, being organized masses of men, trained to obey capable leaders, may overcome the resistance of a people which is far greater in numbers, but unorganized. What are our politics now but organized masses of men, habituated to obey their leaders, among whom to change their vote is stigmatized as the treason of an Arnold, and between which the popular will is driven helplessly from side to side, like a shuttlecock between two battledores? Politics cleans our streets, regulates our education, and so on; it is not to be wondered at that it intrudes into the military sphere, with confidence all the greater because it is there especially ignorant. Let there be no [286] misunderstanding, however. It is perfectly right that the policy of the country should dictate the character and strength of the military establishment; the evil is when policy is controlled by ignorance, summed up in a mistaken but captivating catchword—"for defence only."

Among all masters of military art—including therein naval art—it is a thoroughly accepted principle that mere defensive war means military ruin, and therefore national disaster. It is vain to maintain a military or naval force whose power is not equal to assuming the offensive soon or late; which cannot, first or last, go out, assail the enemy, and hurt him in his vital interests. A navy for defence only, in the *political* sense, means a navy that will only be used in case we are forced into war; a navy for defence only, in the *military* sense, means a navy that can only await attack and defend its own, leaving the enemy at ease as regards his own interests, and at liberty to choose his own time and manner of fighting.

It is to be observed also that the most beneficial use of a military force is not to *wage* war, however successfully, but to *prevent* war, with all its suffering, expense, and complication of [287] embarrassments. Of course, therefore, a navy for defence only, from which an enemy need fear no harm, is of small account in diplomatic relations, for it is nearly useless as a deterrent from war.

Whatever there may be in our conditions otherwise to prevent states from attacking us, a navy "for defence only" will not add to them. For mere harbor defence, fortifications are decisively superior to ships, except where peculiar local conditions are found. All our greatest cities on the Atlantic and Gulf coasts can be locally defended better by forts than by ships; but if, instead of a navy "for defence only," there be one so large that the enemy must send a great many ships across the Atlantic, if he sends any, then the question whether he can spare so great a number is very serious, considering the ever-critical condition of European politics. Suppose, for instance, we could put twenty battleships in commission for war in thirty days, and that we had threatening trouble with either Germany, France, Great Britain, or Russia. There is not one of these, except Great Britain, that could afford to send over here twenty-five battleships, which would be the very fewest needed, seeing the [288] distance of their operations from home; while Great Britain, relying wholly on her navy for the integrity of her empire, equally cannot afford the hostility of a nation having twenty battleships, and with whom her points of difference are as inconsequential to her as they are with us.

It should be remembered, too, that any war which may arise with the naval nations of Europe—or with Japan, which will soon rank with them—will not be with reference to our own territories, but to our external relations. In the Monroe doctrine, as now understood and viewed in the light of the Venezuela incident, with the utterances then made by our statesmen of all parties, we have on hand one of the biggest contracts any modern state has undertaken. Nor may we anticipate from other nations the easy acquiescence of Great Britain. The way the latter sticks by Canada should warn us that we prevailed in Venezuela because the matter to her was not worth war. Great Britain is gorged with land. Her statesmen are weary of looking after it, and of the persistence with which one advance compels another. It is not so with Germany and [289] France. The latter is traditionally our friend, however, and her ambitions, even when she held Canada, have ever pointed east rather than west. But how about Germany? It is the fashion here to proclaim the Emperor a fool, for his shibboleth is imperialistic and not republican; but if he be, it is with the folly of the age on the European Continent—the hunger for ships, colonies, and commerce, after which the great Napoleon so hankered, and upon which the prosperity of Great Britain has been built.

Ships, colonies, commerce, mean to a European nation of to-day just what our vast, half-improved, heavily tariffed territory means to us. They mean to those nations room to expand, land wherewith to portion off the sons and daughters that cannot find living space at home, widespread political and international influence, through blood affiliation with prosperous colonies, the power of which, in the sentiment of brotherhood, received such illustration in the Queen's Jubilee—one of the most majestic sights of the ages; for no Roman triumph ever equalled for variety of interest the Jubilee, in which not victorious force, but love, [290] the all-powerful, was the tie that knit the diversities of the great pageant into one coherent, living whole. What political power is stable save that which holds men's hearts? And what holds men's hearts like blood-relationship, permitted free course and given occasional manifestation and exchange? German colonies, like unto those of Great Britain—such is the foolish day-dream of the German Emperor, if folly it be; but if he be a fool, he knows at least that reciprocal advantage, reciprocal interests, promote the exchange of kindly offices, by which has been kept alive the love between Englishmen at home and Englishmen in the colonies. He knows, also, that such advantages derive from power, from force—not force exerted necessarily but force possessed—and that force, power, depends not upon fleets and armies only, but upon positions also—war being, as Napoleon used to say, "a business of positions"—one of those pregnant phrases of the great captain upon which a man may meditate many hours without exhausting it. A state that aims at maritime power and at colonial empire, as Germany unquestionably—nay, avowedly—now does, needs not [291] only large and widely dispersed colonies; she further needs influence upon those routes of commerce which connect together countries and colonies, and for that she wants possession of minor points, whose value is rather military than commercial, but which essentially affect the control of the sea and of the communications.

Now the secrets of the Emperor and of his more confidential advisers are not all worn upon the sleeve, as might be inferred from the audacity and apparent imprudence of occasional utterances. It is known, however, not only from his words, which might be discounted, but from his acts, that he wants a big navy, that he has meddled in South Africa, and that he has on a slight prbook, but not, it may well be believed, in any frivolous spirit, seized Kiao-chou, in China. What all this means to himself can be only a matter of inference. The present writer, after inquiring in quarters likely to be well informed, has been able to obtain nothing more positive than deductions, reasonably made, by men whose business it is to watch current events in Europe; but the idea has long been forming in the minds of political thinkers, [292] looking not only upon the moves of the political chess-board as they superficially appear in each day's news, and are dictated largely by momentary emergencies, but seeking also to detect the purpose and temperament of the players—be they men in power or national tendencies—that the German Emperor is but continuing and expanding a scheme of policy inherited from his predecessors in the government of the state. Nay, more; it is thought that this policy represents a tendency and a need of the German people itself, in the movement towards national unity between its racial constituents, in which so great an advance has already been accomplished in the last thirty years. Elements long estranged, but of the same blood, can in no way more surely attain to community of interest and of view than by the development of an external policy, of which the benefits and the pride may be common to all. True unity requires some common object, around which diverse interests may cling and crystallize. Nations, like families, need to look outside themselves, if they would escape, on the one hand, narrow self-satisfaction, or, on the other, pitiful internal dissensions. The [293] far-reaching external activities fostered in Great Britain by her insular position have not only intensified patriotism, but have given also a certain nobility of breadth to her statesmanship up to the middle of this century.

Why, then, should not Germany, whose political unity was effected near two centuries after that of Great Britain, do wisely in imitating a policy whereby the older state has become an empire, that still travels onward to a further and greater unity, which, if realized, shall embrace in one fold remote quarters of the world? Where is the folly of the one conception or of the other? The folly, if it prove such, has as yet no demonstrable existence, save in the imaginations of a portion of the people of the United States, who, clinging to certain maxims of a century ago—when they were quite applicable—or violently opposed to any active interest in matters outside our family of States, find that those who differ from themselves are, if Americans, jingoes, and if foreigners, like the present Emperor William and Mr. Chamberlain, fools. The virtues and the powers of the British and German peoples may prove unequal to their ambitions—time alone can show; [294] but it is a noble aim in their rulers to seek to extend their influence, to establish their positions, and to knit them together, in such wise that as races they may play a mighty part in the world's history. The ambition is noble, even if it fail; if it succeed, our posterity may take a different view of its folly, and of our own wisdom in this generation.

For there are at least two steps, in other directions than those as yet taken, by which the Emperor, when he feels strong enough at sea—he is yet scarcely in middle life—might greatly and suddenly increase the maritime empire of Germany, using means which are by no means unprecedented, historically, but which would certainly arouse vehement wrath in the United States, and subject to a severe test our maxim of a navy for defence only. There is a large and growing German colony in southern Brazil, and I am credibly informed that there is a distinct effort to divert thither, by means direct and indirect, a considerable part of the emigration which now comes to the United States, and therefore is lost politically to Germany—for she has, of course, no prospect of colonization here. The inference is that the [295] Emperor hopes at a future day, for which he is young enough to wait, to find in southern Brazil a strong German population, which in due time may seek to detach itself from the Brazilian Republic, as Texas once detached itself from Mexico; and which may then seek political union with Germany, as Texas sought political union with the United States, to obtain support against her former owners and masters. Without advancing any particular opinion as to the advisable geographical limits of the Monroe doctrine, we may be pretty sure that the American people would wordily resent an act which in our press would be called "the aggression of a European military monarchy upon the political or territorial rights of an American republic." This also could be accompanied with the liberal denunciation of William II. which now ornaments our editorial columns; but hard words break no bones, and the practical question would remain, "What are you going to do about it?" with a navy "for defence only." If you cannot offend Germany, in the military sense of "offend"—that is, if you cannot seek her out and *hurt* her—how are you going to control her? In [296] contemplation of the future contingencies of our national policy, let us contrast our own projected naval force with that now recommended to the German Reichstag by the Budget Committee, despite the many prophecies that the Emperor could not obtain his desired navy. "The Budget Committee of the Reichstag to-day adopted, in accordance with the government proposals, parts of the naval bill, fixing the number of ships to be held in readiness for service as follows: 1 flagship, 18 battleships, 12 large cruisers, 30 small cruisers, 8 coast-defence ironclads, and 13 gunboats, besides torpedo-boats, schoolships, and small gunboats." [5] That these numbers were fixed with reference to the United States is indeed improbable; but the United States should take note.

A second means of expanding Germany as a colonial power would be to induce the Dutch—who are the Germans of the lower Rhine and the North Sea—to seek union with the German Empire, the empire of the Germans of the upper Rhine, of the Elbe, and of the Baltic. This, it may be said, would be far less difficult in consummation than the scheme last s [297] uggested; for in Brazil, as in the United States and elsewhere, the German emigrant tends to identify himself with the institutions he finds around him, and shows little disposition to political independence—a fact which emphasizes the necessity of strictly German colonies, if the race, outside of Europe, is not to undergo political absorption. The difficulties or the advantages which the annexation of Holland might involve, as regards the political balance of power in Europe, and the vast Asiatic colonies of the Dutch—Sumatra, Java, New Guinea, etc.—are a consideration outside the present scope of American policy; but the transaction would involve one little incident as to which, unlike southern Brazil, a decided opinion may be expressed, and that incident would be the transference of the island of Curaçao, in the West Indies, to Germany. If Curaçao and its political tenure do not fall within the purview of the Monroe doctrine, the Monroe doctrine has no existence; for the island, though small, has a wellnigh impregnable harbor, and lies close beside the routes to the Central American Isthmus, which is to us what Egypt and Suez are to England. But what [298] objection can we urge, or what can we do, with a navy "for defence only," in the military sense of the word "defence"?

The way out of this confusion of thought, the logical method of reconciling the political principle of non-aggression with a naval power capable of taking the offensive, if necessary, is to recognize, and to say, that defence means not merely defence of our territory, but defence of our just national interests, whatever they be and wherever they are. For example, the exclusion of direct European political control from the Isthmus of Panama is as really a matter of national defence as is the protection of New York Harbor. Take this as the political meaning of the phrase "a navy for defence only," and naval men, I think, must admit that it is no longer inapplicable as a military phrase, but expresses adequately the naval needs of the nation. But no military student can consider efficient a force so limited, in quantity or in quality, that it must await attack before it can act.

Now admitting this view as to the scope of the word "defence," what is the best method of defending your interests when you know that [299] another intends to attack them? Is it to busy yourself with precautions here, and precautions there, in every direction, to head him off when he comes? Or is it to take the simpler means of so preparing that you have the power to hurt him, and to make him afraid that, if he moves, he will be the worse hurt of the two? In life generally a man who means mischief is kept in check best by fear of being hurt; if he has no more to dread than failure to do harm, no reason to apprehend receiving harm, he will make his attempt. But while this is probably true of life in general, it is notably true of warfare. The state which in war relies simply upon defending itself, instead of upon hurting the enemy, is bound to incur disaster, and for the very simple reason that the party which proposes to strike a blow has but one thing to do; whereas he who proposes only to ward off blows has a dozen things, for he cannot know upon which interest, of a dozen that he may have, the coming blow may fall. For this reason, again, a "navy for defence only" is a wholly misleading phrase, unless defence be construed to include *all* national interests, and not only the national territory; and further, [300] unless it be understood that the best defence of one's own interests is power to injure those of the enemy.

In the summary of points to be dealt with has been included the opinion that offensive action by a navy may be limited to merely preying upon the enemy's commerce—that being considered not only a real injury, but one great enough to bring him to peace. Concerning this, it will suffice here to say that national maritime commerce does not consist in a number of ships sprinkled, as by a pepper-pot, over the surface of the ocean. Rightly viewed, it constitutes a great system, with the strength and weakness of such. Its strength is that possessed by all organized power, namely, that it can undergo a good deal of local injury, such as scattered cruisers may inflict, causing inconvenience and suffering, without receiving vital harm. A strong man cannot be made to quit his work by sticking pins in him, or by bruising his shins or blacking his eyes; he must be hit in a vital part, or have a bone broken, to be laid up. The weaknesses of commerce—the fatally vulnerable parts of its system—are the commercial routes over which ships pass. They [301] are the bones, the skeleton, the framework of the organism. Hold them, break them, and commerce falls with a crash, even though no ship is taken, but all locked up in safe ports. But to effect this is not the work of dispersed cruisers picking up ships here and there, as birds pick up crumbs, but of vessels massed into powerful fleets, holding the sea, or at the least making the highways too dangerous for use. A navy so planned is for defence indeed, in the true sense that the best defence is to crush your enemy by depriving him of the use of the sea.

We now come to the assertion that if the United States takes to itself interests beyond the sea—of which Hawaii is an instance—it not only adds to its liabilities, which is true, but incurs an unnecessary exposure, to guard against which we need no less than the greatest navy in the world.

It might be retorted that, willy-nilly, we already, by general national consent, have accepted numerous external interests—embraced under the Monroe doctrine; and that, as regards Hawaii, many even who reject annexation admit that our interests will not tolerate any other nation taking those islands. But how [302] shall we enforce even that limited amount of interest if any other power—Great Britain, Germany, or Japan—decide to take, and the islanders acquiesce? In such cases we should even be worse off, militarily, than with annexation completed. Let us, however, put aside this argument—of the many already existing external interests—and combat this allegation, that an immense navy would be needed, by recurring to the true military conception of defence already developed. The subject will thus tend to unity of treatment, centring round that word "defence." Effective defence does not consist primarily in power to protect, but in power to injure. A man's defence against a snake, if cornered—if he must have to do with it—is not to protect himself, but to kill the snake. If a snake got into the room, as often happens in India, the position should not be estimated by ability to get out of the room one's self, but by power to get rid of the snake. In fact, a very interesting illustration of the true theory of defence is found in a casual remark in a natural history about snakes—that comparatively few are dangerous to man, but that the whole family is protected by the fear [303] those few inspire. If attacked by a dog, safety is not sought chiefly in the means of warding him off, but by showing him the means possessed of hurting him, as by picking up a stone; and with a man, where an appeal lies to the intelligence, the argument from power to injure is peculiarly strong. If a burglar, thinking to enter a room, knows that he may—or will—kill the occupant, but that the latter may break his leg, he will not enter. The game would not be worth the candle.

Apply this thought now to the United States and its naval needs. As Great Britain is by very far the greatest naval power, let us take her to be the supposed enemy. If we possessed the Hawaiian Islands, and war unhappily broke out with Great Britain, she could now, if she desired, take them without trouble, so far as our navy is concerned; so could France; so possibly, five years hence, could Japan. That is, under our present conditions of naval weakness, either France or Great Britain could spare ships enough to overcome our force, without fatally crippling her European fleet; whereas, were our navy half the size of the British, she could not afford to send half her fleet so far [304] away from home; nor, if we had half ours in the Pacific and half in the Atlantic, could she afford to send one-third or one-fourth of her entire navy so far from her greater interests, independent of the fact that, even if victorious, it would be very badly used before our force was defeated. Hawaii is not worth that to Great Britain; whereas it is of so much consequence to us that, even if lost, it would probably be returned at a peace, as Martinique and Guadeloupe invariably have been to France. Great Britain would not find its value equivalent to our resentment at her holding it. Now the argument as to the British fleet is still stronger as to France, for she is as distant as Great Britain and has a smaller navy. The argument is different as regards Japan, for she is nearer by far than they, only half as far again as we, and that power has recently given us an intimation which, if we disregard, we do so in face of the facts. Her remonstrance about the annexation of Hawaii, however far it went, gave us fair warning that a great naval state was about to come into being in the Pacific, prepared to watch, and perhaps to contest, our action in what we thought our [305] interests demanded. From that instant the navy of Japan becomes a standard, showing, whether we annex the islands or not, a minimum beneath which our Pacific fleet cannot be allowed to fall, without becoming a "navy for defence only," in the very worst sense.

This brief train of reasoning will suggest why it is not necessary to have a navy equal to the greatest, in order to insure that sense of fear which deters a rival from war, or handicaps his action in war. The biggest navy that ever existed cannot all be sent on one mission, in any probable state of the political world. A much smaller force, favorably placed, produces an effect far beyond its proportionate numbers; for, to quote again Napoleon's phrase, "War is a business of positions." This idea is by no means new, even to unprofessional men; on the contrary, it is so old that it is deplorable to see such fatuous arguments as the necessity of equalling Great Britain's navy adduced against any scheme of external policy. The annexation of Hawaii, to recur to that, may be bad policy for many reasons, of which I am no good judge; but, as a naval student, I hesitate not to say that, while annexation *may* [306] entail a bigger navy than is demanded for the mere exclusion of other states from the islands—though I personally do not think so—it is absurd to say that we should need a navy equal to that of Great Britain. In 1794 Gouverneur Morris wrote that if the United States had twenty ships of the line in commission, no other state would provoke her enmity. At that time Great Britain's navy was relatively more powerful than it is now, while she and France were rivalling each other in testing the capacity of our country to stand kicking; but Morris's estimate was perfectly correct, and shows how readily a sagacious layman can understand a military question, if only he will put his mind to it, and not merely echo the press. Great Britain then could not—and much more France could not—afford to have twenty ships of the line operating against her interests on the other side of the Atlantic. They could not afford it in actual war; they could not afford it even in peace, because not only might war arise at any time, but it would be much more likely to happen if either party provoked the United States to hostility. The mere menace of such a force, its mere existence, [307] would have insured decent treatment without war; and Morris, who was an able financier, conjectured that to support a navy of such size for twenty years would cost the public treasury less than five years of war would,—not to mention the private losses of individuals in war.

All policy that involves external action is sought to be discredited by this assertion, that it entails the expense of a navy equal to the greatest now existing on the sea, no heed being given to the fact that we already have assumed such external responsibilities, if any weight is to be attached to the evident existence of a strong popular feeling in favor of the Monroe doctrine, or to Presidential or Congressional utterances in the Venezuela business, or in that of Hawaii. The assertion is as old as the century; as is also the complementary ignorance of the real influence of an inferior military or naval force in contemporary policy, when such force either is favored by position, or can incline decisively, to one side or the other, the scales in a doubtful balance. To such misapprehensions we owed, in the early part of this century, the impressment of hundreds of American seamen, and the despotic control [308] of our commerce by foreign governments; to this, the blockading of our coasts, the harrying of the shores of Chesapeake Bay, the burning of Washington, and a host of less remembered attendant evils. All these things might have been prevented by the timely maintenance of a navy of tolerable strength, deterring the warring powers from wanton outrage.

In the present day the argument that none but the greatest navy is of any avail, and that such is too expensive for us to contemplate—as it probably is—is re-enforced by the common statement that the ship built to-day becomes obsolete in an extremely short time, the period stated being generally a rhetorical figure rather than an exact estimate. The word "obsolete" itself is used here vaguely. Strictly, it means no more than "gone out of use;" but it is understood, correctly, I think, to mean "become useless." A lady's bonnet may become obsolete, being gone out of use because no longer in fashion, though it may still be an adequate head-covering; but an obsolete ship of war can only be one that is put out of use because it is useless. A ship momentarily out of use, because not needed, is no more obsolete than [309] a hat hung up when the owner comes in. When a ship is called obsolete, therefore, it is meant that she is out of use for the same reason that many old English words are—because they are no longer good for their purpose; their meaning being lost to mankind in general, they no longer serve for the exchange of thought.

In this sense the obsolescence of modern ships of war is just one of those half-truths which, as Tennyson has it, are ever the worst of lies; it is harder to meet and fight outright than an unqualified untruth. It is true that improvement is continually going on in the various parts of the complex mechanism which constitutes a modern ship of war; although it is also true that many changes are made which are not improvements, and that reversion to an earlier type, the abandonment of a once fancied improvement, is no unprecedented incident in recent naval architecture and naval ordnance. The revulsion from the monitor, the turreted ship pure and simple, to the broadside battery analogous to that carried by the old ships of Farragut and Nelson, is one of the most singular and interesting changes in [310] men's thoughts that the writer has met, either in his experience or in his professional reading. The day can be recalled when the broadside battleship was considered as dead as Cock-Robin—her knell was rung, and herself buried without honors; yet, not only has she revived, but I imagine that I should have a very respectable following among naval officers now in believing, as I do, that the broadside guns, and not those in the turrets, are the primary battery of the ship—primary, I mean, in fighting value. Whatever the worth of this opinion,—which is immaterial to the present contention,—a change so radical as from broadside battery to turreted ships, and from the latter back to broadside, though without entirely giving up turrets, should cause some reasonable hesitancy in imputing obsoleteness to any armored steamship. The present battleship reproduces, in essential principles, the ships that preceded the epoch-making monitor—the pivot guns of the earlier vessels being represented by the present turrets, and their broadsides by the present broadside. The prevalence of the monitor type was an interlude, powerfully affecting the [311] development of navies, but making nothing obsolete. It did not effect a revolution, but a modification—much as homœopathy did in the "regular practice."

There is, of course, a line on one side of which the term "obsolete" applies, but it may be said that no ship is obsolete for which fighting-work can be found, with a tolerable chance—a fighting chance—of her being successful; because, though unequal to this or that position of exposure, she, by occupying an inferior one, releases a better ship. And here again we must guard ourselves from thinking that inferior force—inferior in number or inferior in quality—has *no* chance against a superior. The idea is simply another phase of "a navy equal to the greatest," another military heresy. A ship under the guns of one thrice her force, from which her speed cannot carry her, is doubtless a lost ship. She may be called even obsolete, though she be the last product of naval science, just from a dock-yard. Before such extreme conditions are reached, however, by a ship or a fleet, many other factors than merely relative force come into play; primarily, man, with all that his personality [312] implies—skill, courage, discipline,—after that, chance, opportunity, accidents of time, accidents of place, accidents of ground,—the whole unforeseeable chapter of incidents which go to form military history. A military situation is made up of many factors, and before a ship can be called obsolete, useless to the great general result, it must be determined that she can contribute no more than zero to either side of the equation—or of the inequality. From the time she left the hands of the designers, a unit of maximum value, throughout the period of her gradual declension, many years will elapse during which a ship once first-rate will be an object of consideration to friend and foe. She will wear out like a garment, but she does not necessarily become obsolete till worn out. It may be added that the indications now are that radical changes of design are not to be expected shortly, and that we have reached a type likely to endure. A ship built five years hence may have various advantages of detail over one now about to be launched, but the chances are they will not be of a kind that reverse the odds of battle. This, of course, is only a forecast, not an [313] assertion; a man who has witnessed the coming and going of the monitor type will forbear prophecy.

Now, as always, the best ships in the greatest number, as on shore the best troops in the greatest masses, will be carried as speedily as possible, and maintained as efficiently as possible, on the front of operations. But in various directions and at various points behind that front there are other interests to be subserved, by vessels of inferior class, as garrisons may be made up wholly or in part of troops no longer well fitted for the field. But should disaster occur, or the foe prove unexpectedly strong, the first line of reserved ships will move forward to fill the gaps, analogous in this to the various corps of reserved troops who have passed their first youth, with which the Continental organizations of military service have made us familiar. This possibility has been recognized so well by modern naval men that some even have looked for decisive results, not at the hands of the first and most powerful ships, but from the readiness and number of those which have passed into the reserve, and will come into play after the first [314] shock of war. That a reserve force should decide a doubtful battle or campaign is a frequent military experience—an instance of superior staying power.

There is no reason, therefore, to worry about a ship becoming obsolete, any more than there is over the fact that the best suit of to-day may be that for the office next year, and may finally descend to a dependent, or be cut down for a child. Whatever money a nation is willing to spend on maintaining its first line of ships, it is not weaker, but stronger, when one of these drops into the reserve and is replaced by a newer ship. The great anxiety, in truth, is not lest the ships should not continue valid, but lest there be not trained men enough to man both the first line and the reserve.

Here the present article, as at first contemplated, would have closed; but the recent disaster to the *Maine* has produced its own crop of sudden and magnified apprehensions. These, to the professional mind, are necessarily a matter of concern, but chiefly because they have showed the seeds of a popular distrust before sown in men's minds. As evinced, [315] however, they too are fallacies born of imperfect knowledge. The magnitude of the calamity was indisputable; but the calm self-possession of the nation and of the better portion of the press, face to face with the possible international troubles that might ensue, contrasted singularly with the unreasoned imaginations that immediately found voice concerning the nature and dangers of battleships. The political self-possession and dignity reposed upon knowledge—not, indeed, of the eventual effect upon our international relations—but knowledge, bred of long acquaintance with public affairs, that, before further action, there must be investigation; and that after investigation, action, if it must follow, would be taken with due deliberation. So men were content to wait for justice to pursue its even course.

But the fact that such an appalling catastrophe had befallen one battleship fell upon the minds imperfectly informed in naval matters, and already possessed by various exaggerated impressions, loosely picked up from time to time. Men knew not what to think, and so thought the worst—as we are all apt [316] to do when in the dark. It is possible that naval officers, being accustomed to live over a magazine, and ordinarily to eat their meals within a dozen yards of the powder, may have a too great, though inevitable, familiarity with the conditions. There is, however, no contempt for them among us; and the precautions taken are so well known, the remoteness of danger so well understood, that it is difficult to comprehend the panic terror that found utterance in the remarks of some men, presumably well informed on general matters. It is evidently a very long and quite illogical step to infer that, because the results of an accident may be dreadful, therefore the danger of the accident occurring at all is very great. On land, a slight derangement of a rail, a slight obstacle on a track, the breaking of a wheel or of an axle, may plunge a railroad train to frightful disaster; but we know from annual experience that while such accidents do happen, and sometimes with appalling consequences, the chance of their happening in a particular case is so remote that we disregard it. At sea, every day of every year for centuries back, a couple of hundred warships—to speak [317] moderately—have been traversing the ocean or lying in port, like the *Maine*, with abundance of powder on board; and for the last quarter of a century very many of these have been, and now are, essentially of the type of that unfortunate vessel. The accident that befell her, if its origin be precisely determined, may possibly impose some further precaution not hitherto taken; but whatever the cause may prove to have been, it is clear that the danger of such an event happening is at no time great, because it is almost, if not quite, unprecedented among the great number of warships now continuously in service. Similarly, on the seas, the disasters to the *Ville du Havre*, to the *Oregon*, and, only three years ago, to the *Elbe*, show the terrific results of collision, to which every ship crossing the ocean is liable. Collisions between vessels less known than those named are of weekly occurrence. Yet no general outcry is raised against the general safety of the transatlantic liners. People unconsciously realize that, where accidents are so infrequent, the risk to themselves in the individual case is slight, though the results, when they happen, are dreadful. Men know [318] instinctively that the precautions taken must be practically adequate, or safety would not be the almost universal rule which it is.

It should be remembered, too, that the present battleship is not a sudden invention, springing up in a night, like Jonah's gourd, or newly contrived by a council sitting for the purpose, like a brand-new Constitution of the French Revolution. The battleship of to-day is the outcome of a gradual evolution extending over forty years. Its development has been governed by experience, showing defects or suggesting improvements; and the entire process has been superintended by men of the highest practical and scientific intelligence, naval architects and seamen, constantly exchanging ideas, not only with their own countrymen, but, through the scientific publications of the day, with the whole world. What Ruskin said of the old ship of the line is still more true of the modern battleship: no higher exhibition of man's creative faculties is probably anywhere to be found. In view, therefore, of its genesis, and of the practical results of yearly cruisings, the battleship in its service of peace is entitled to the confidence we give to the work of [319] competent men in all departments; nor should that confidence be withdrawn because of a single occurrence, if the *Maine* prove to have fallen victim to internal accident. If, on the other hand, her destruction proceeded from an external cause,—that is, if she fell as ships fall in war,—it may safely be said that, in actions between ships, no means of injury now in use on shipboard could effect the instantaneous and widespread destruction manifested in her case, unless by a shell finding its way to her magazine. This is a remote possibility, though it exists; but when it comes to fighting, men must remember that it is not possible to make war without running risks, and that it is highly improbable that one-tenth as many seamen will die from the explosion of their own magazines, so occasioned, as from the direct blow of the enemy's projectiles.

Note.—Since this article was written, in January, 1898, it has become known that the attitude of Japan towards the United States, regarded as a power of the Pacific, has been reversed, and that—as already remarked in the preface to this volume—her leading statesmen, instead of resenting the annexation of Hawaii, now welcome cordially the advance of the United States to the Philippines. This change, occurring as it has within four years, affords a [320] striking indication of the degree to which the attention of mankind has been aroused by the character of Russia's progress in northeastern Asia, and upon the Pacific, as well as of the influence thereby exerted upon the currents of men's thoughts, and upon international relations.

FOOTNOTES:

[5] From a telegram from Berlin of March 2, 1898.

Uniform with "Lessons of the War with Spain and Other Articles."

THE INTEREST OF AMERICA IN
SEA POWER, Present and Future.

By Capt. A.T. Mahan . With two maps showing strategic points. Crown 8vo. Cloth, gilt top. $2.00.

CONTENTS
I. The United States Looking Outward.
II. Hawaii and our Sea Power.
III. The Isthmus and our Sea Power.
IV. Anglo-American Alliance.
V. The Future in Relation to American Naval Power.
VI. Preparedness for Naval War.
VII. A Twentieth Century Outlook.
VIII. Strategic Features of the Gulf of Mexico and the Caribbean Sea.

All the civilized world knows Captain Mahan is an expert on naval matters. His present position on the Board of Strategy, directing the American fleets, has made him even more conspicuous than usual. These papers, in the light of the present war, prove Captain Mahan a most sane and sure prophet. It seems hard to imagine any topics more fascinating at the present time. No romance, no novel, could possibly equal such essays as these, by such an author, in present public interest. So many of his theories have come to reality as to be positively remarkable.—*The Criterion.*

The last paper, "Strategic Features of the Caribbean Sea and the Gulf of Mexico," written only last year, deals with problems that now confront the people of the United States in the shape of practical questions that will have to be decided for the present and the future. It is well within the bounds of truth to say that an intelligent comprehension of these questions is not possible without a reading of the present volume.—*Philadelphia Inquirer.*

His paper on Hawaii is timely at this moment, as it treats of the annexation of the Sandwich Islands from the point of view which our statesmen might well take, rather than from the professional view which a naval officer might be expected to hold.—*Philadelphia Telegraph.*

The substance of all these essays concerns every intelligent voter in this country.—*Boston Herald.*

LITTLE, BROWN, & COMPANY,
Publishers
254 Washington Street, Boston.

THE INFLUENCE OF SEA POWER
UPON HISTORY, 1660-1783.

By Capt. A.T. Mahan. With 25 charts illustrative of great naval battles. 8vo. Cloth, gilt top. $4.00.

Captain Mahan has been recognized by all competent judges, not merely as the most distinguished living writer on naval strategy, but as the originator and first exponent of what may be called the philosophy of naval history.—*London Times.*

No book of recent publication has been received with such enthusiasm of grateful admiration as that written by an officer of the American Navy, Captain Mahan, upon Sea Power and Naval Achievements. It simply supplants all other books on the subject, and takes its place in our libraries as the standard work.— Dean Hole , in "*More Memories.*"

An altogether exceptional work; there is nothing like it in the whole range of naval literature. The work is entirely original in conception, masterful in construction, and scholarly in execution.—*The Critic.*

Captain Mahan, whose name is famous all the world over as that of the author of "The Influence of Sea Power upon History," a work, or rather a series of works, which may fairly be said to have codified the laws of naval strategy. —*The Westminster Gazette.*

An instructive work of the highest value and interest to students and to the reading public, and should find its way into all the libraries and homes of the land.—*Magazine of American History.*

A book that must be read. *First*, it must be read by all schoolmasters, from the head-master of Eton to the head of the humblest board-school in the country. No man is fit to train English boys to fulfil their duties as Englishmen who has not marked, learned, and inwardly digested it. *Secondly*, it must be read by every Englishman and Englishwoman who wishes to be worthy of that name. It is no hard or irksome task to which I call them. The writing is throughout clear, vigorous, and incisive. The book deserves and must attain a world-wide reputation.— Colonel Maurice , *of the British Army, in the "United Service Magazine."*

LITTLE, BROWN, & COMPANY,
Publishers
254 Washington Street, Boston

THE INFLUENCE OF SEA POWER
upon the French Revolution and Empire.

By Capt. A.T. Mahan . With 13 maps and battle plans, 2 vols. 8vo. Cloth, gilt top. $6.00.

A highly interesting and an important work, having lessons and suggestions which are calculated to be of high value to the people of the United States. His pages abound with spirited and careful accounts of the great naval battles and manœuvres which occurred during the period treated.—*New York Tribune.*

Captain Mahan has done more than to write a new book upon naval history. He has even done more than to write the best book that has ever been written upon naval history, though he has done this likewise; for he has written a book which may be regarded as founding a new school of naval historical writing. Captain Mahan's volumes are already accepted as the standard authorities of their kind, not only here, but in England and in Europe generally. It should be a matter of pride to all Americans that an officer of our own navy should have written such books.— Theodore Roosevelt , in "*Political Science Quarterly.*"

THE LIFE OF NELSON: The Embodiment
of the Sea Power of Great Britain.

By Capt. A.T. Mahan . With 19 portraits and plates in photogravure and 21 maps and battle plans. 2 vols. 8vo. Cloth, gilt top. $8.00.

Captain Mahan's work will become one of the greatest naval classics.—*London Times.*

The greatest literary achievement of the author of "The Influence of Sea Power upon History." Never before have charm of style, perfect professional knowledge, the insight and balanced judgment of a great historian, and deep admiration for the hero been blended in any biography of Nelson.—*London Standard.*

LITTLE, BROWN, & COMPANY,
Publishers
254 Washington Street, Boston

CAPTAIN MAHAN'S LIFE OF NELSON

NEW POPULAR EDITION
COMPLETE IN ONE VOLUME

THE LIFE OF NELSON. The Embodiment
of the Sea Power of Great Britain.

By Capt. A.T. Mahan . With 12 portraits and plates in half-tone and a photogravure frontispiece. Crown 8vo. Cloth. 750 pages, $3.00.

It is not astonishing that this standard life is already passing into a new edition. It has simply displaced all its predecessors except one, that of Southey, which is the vade-mecum of British patriotism, a stimulant of British loyalty, literature of high quality, but in no sense a serious historical or psychological study. The reader will find in this book three things; an unbroken series of verified historical facts related in minute detail; a complete picture of the hero, with every virtue justly estimated but with no palliation of weakness or fault; and lastly a triumphant vindication of a theses novel and startling to most, that the earth's barriers are continental, its easy ad defensible highways those of the trackless ocean. Captain Mahan has revealed the modern world to itself.— *American Historical Review, July, 1899.*

Captain Mahan's masterly life of Nelson has already taken its place as the final book on the subject.—*Mail and Express*, New York.

One never tires of reading or reflecting upon the marvellous career of Horatio Nelson, the greatest sea captain the world has known. Captain Mahan has written the best biography of Lord Nelson that has yet been given to the world.—*Chicago Evening Post.*

His biography is not merely the best life of Nelson that has ever been written, but it is also perfect, and a model among all the biographies of the world. —*Pall Mall Gazette.*

LITTLE, BROWN, & COMPANY,
Publishers
254, Washington Street, Boston

Typographical errors corrected in text:

Page 31: Reconnoissance replaced with Reconnaissance
Page 297: transferrence replaced with transference